Luigi Novelli

Shanghai

Residential Buildings

上海民居

Haiwen Audio-Video Publishers

Contents

Preface

Criteria and Comments *4*

Housing: Residential Buildings in Shanghai *11*

Historical Residence (No. 1) *28*

Progressive Transformation (No. 2-60) *32*

Existing Buildings Roofed In Late 1990s *85*

Appendix 1   Layout Examples *87*

Appendix 2   Housing and Symbols, Living Styles in Shanghai

.... *98*

Bibliography
Language Translation Notes

.... *102*

Acknowledgements

Thanks to Shanghai Book Traders

Special thanks for translation and editing to:
Ms. Claudia Albertini
Ms. Lisa Chisolm
Mr. Eric Lock
Mr. Luo Weiguo
Ms. Daniela Pilia

Preface:

Criteria and Comments

This book is a guide to architecture. This series of guides follows a consistent concept, illustrating buildings with photos, drawings and details of their location in the city. Each structure has the same amount of space devoted to it. Photos are the same size — an exterior view and others showing details or interiors. Text and photos must be explicit: they are not emphatic or vice versa unfavorable.

No personal comments or opinions are included in the guides.

These guides illustrate the architecture and urban landscape in the form of a snapshot from the 1990s to the beginning of the 21st century, which is the period of Shanghai's (second) huge transformation.

Due to the huge scale of the city — 16 million inhabitants — and the large quantity of architecturally interesting buildings, I had to make choices. I needed some guiding criteria.

I followed these criteria: cultural heritage, designers and architects, representativeness, location and dimensions. The result is a combination of all of them.

a) Cultural Heritage: I obtained information about the most interesting buildings and those under the protection of the law from books by professors at Tongji University.

b) Designers and architects: Chinese architects, Chinese architectural institutes and foreign architects designed most of the buildings in the city. Other examples lack details of the designers (especially Longtang houses, warehouses, etc.). In some cases, it is not necessary to mention the designers, especially for residential houses.

c) Representativeness: some examples are chosen because they represent a certain theory or trend. Such examples should not be too different from the ideas they are chosen to represent.

d) Location: this is a difficult factor to evaluate. But there is no doubt that buildings in key locations and on main roads — especially public ones — are representative of ideas, concepts and taste. As it was in the past with the waterfront Bund, so it is nowadays with People's Square, Pudong Lujiazui, the Huangpu riverfront, Hongqiao New Area, Xintiandi and other districts that are representative and symbolic of the architecture throughout the city.

e) Dimensions: also difficult to evaluate. But there is no doubt that the dimensions of buildings are representative of ideas, concepts and taste. However, the former RAS Bldg. in

Huqiu Road — one of the smallest buildings documented, located in a remote street — is one of the most interesting buildings in Shanghai. I have also considered and mentioned the Brilliant City beside the Suzhou River.

f) I considered only existing and completed buildings — except for a few under construction. I have not mentioned competitions, projects and other theories.

Since 1992, thanks to my job and this project, I have visited and lived in many residences in Shanghai, both in the Chinese and expatriate communities. Sometimes I rented the houses. I have stayed in the homes of my friends and relatives. I know the living situation in Shanghai and its social and technical problems: the inadequacies of the original construction techniques, overcrowding and the lack of sewage systems. I have seen situations similar to Italy in the 1950s, or London and Paris in the 19th century. Because of my background in history, I don't have — and I must not have — any sentimental feelings about this architecture. I am aware of the great improvements in housing since the 1950s in Shanghai and China. On the other hand, I know of the luxurious and wealthy residences of both Chinese and foreigners, in the past and in the modern day. But such issues are beyond the main topic of this architecture series.

Besides these criteria, the opinions and architectural information included are obviously influenced by my cultural background and my job as an Italian architect (I graduated in my native Rome) and by my private life in Shanghai. These guides are founded mainly on my research about Shanghai since 1997 and my personal experiences in the city since 1992. During the 1990s, I witnessed the rapid transformation of the city, I visited some important buildings when they were under construction — the Grand Theatre, the Jinmao Tower, the Xintiandi Area and the Bank of China in Beijing.

In Shanghai, Western architecture — both in the past and in recent times — is quite different from its roots in Europe and often lacks many elements of its original heritage. Chinese architecture, both traditional and modern, is not my cultural background. The combination of the two is the most interesting — and historically significant — aspect of Shanghai, and the most original and innovative aspect of this city's development.

Due to my background and experiences, the guides will focus primarily on the mixture of Chinese and Western architecture in Shanghai.

Luigi Novelli
Shanghai, September 2002

Shanghai Residential Buildings

◄ Lujiazui Residence

▼ Shikumen Gates

*S*hanghai Residential Buildings

Shikumen Roofs and Windows

*S*hanghai Residential Buildings

Shanghai Residential Buildings

Shikumen Houses Renovated in 1990s for New Functions Inside

*S*hanghai Residential Buildings

Housing built in 1990s mixed with those built in 1960s and 1970s (reroofed in 1990s)

Preface:

Housing: Residential Buildings in Shanghai

Shanghai is one of the most populous cities in the world — 15 or 16 million inhabitants — and also one of the most densely populated cities. Housing is a key concern in such a situation involving different aspects: social, residential, technical, architectural, all of which should be considered in light of the different historical and political periods in which the housing was created.

From the end of the 19th century, during the foreign concession period both under the Qing Dynasty and the Republican period, through the Japanese occupation, and from Liberation in 1949 until the beginning of 21st century when China entered the WTO, many different social situations have occurred. Of course, these different periods greatly influenced the style of housing and residential buildings throughout the city.

Different concepts have been used to solve the housing problem. And the concept adopted depends upon the nature of the project — low quality / high quantity or luxury housing, private or government investors, different techniques. Concepts, some traditional and some experimental, were adopted from Chinese traditions, Western traditions or a mixture of many. Chinese architects, university institutes, government institutes, oversea Chinese architects as well as Western architects have all participated in the design of such projects.

An original concept was adopted and became the most popular and widely used in the city: the Longtang houses. This original housing style was conceived in Shanghai.

The density rate of Shanghai's population was once the highest in the world: about 4 square meters per person. Many residential buildings were overcrowded, up to even double or more of their designed capacity. The quality, the techniques and the style of construction were irrelevant — there were simply more families in the buildings than was originally planned. Often there was one family for each room, and they shared the facilities — bathroom and kitchen — with other families. This situation existed throughout the city: in the Old Town, along the Suzhou River, in the Longtang houses, in the apartments' buildings, in the semi-detached houses. This happened with the great population increase and development of the city in the 1930s and, again, in the 1950s.

Since the 1950s, the city witnessed great advances in solving its housing problems. Many residential areas — estates — have been designed and built by the government and public institutes. New buildings — built to house the residents moved from the overcrowded areas — occupied new land in the suburbs.

In the city center, the existing old houses — Longtang, semi-detached, intensive residential blocks and even villas — are still overcrowded even today. They also suffer from structural problems related to the inadequacy of the original construction and lack of a sewage system. Some of them have been internally renovated with sanitary facilities introduced, some of them have been re-painted on the exterior and re-roofed. Some have been converted to other functions and structures. But most of the old housing is still in poor condition.

Since the beginning of the 1990s — during the transformation of Shanghai — a huge quantity of new residential complexes, including high-rises, 6-7 storied buildings and villas, have been built. Many are still under construction, and many others are planned for the next few years. These complexes are found both in the center of the city and in the suburbs, in former industrial areas and in the countryside.

Since the first decades of the 20th century, the concepts adopted come mainly from the West: semi-detached houses, apartments and villas. The most interesting question is whether and how these concepts change as a result of their contact with Chinese tradition. Longtang houses — from the end of 18th century to the 1940s — are the best representative of the mixture between Western and Chinese housing concepts: this is the reason for their importance. Single dwelling concepts changed from Longtang houses — still deeply rooted in the Chinese tradition (courtyard type) — to modern residential complexes much influenced by Western and modern international ideas (multi-apartment building).

Since the 1950s, the dimensions of single apartments have changed. Originally they were built without a private bathroom, while in modern complexes, each apartment is equipped with at least one bathroom, a kitchen, two/three or more bedrooms, balconies and heating system. In these complexes the resident density could be about 20 square meters per person or less.

At the beginning of 1990s, the density rate was less than 4 square meters per resident. The city's target is 8-10 square meters per resident. Although a huge quantity of new residential buildings were built in the 1990s (and more under construction), the density rate is still high. Even now, many areas — the Old Chinese city in the formerly Nanshi District, the north side of Suzhou River in Zhabei and Putuo District — suffer overcrowding problems.

From the 1950s to the late 1990s, the site plan of these complexes changed too. New ideas influenced both Longtang houses and residential areas site plans, based on research into better quality living environments. The same concept could have more or less public space and green areas. In the new projects, even the positioning of the buildings is different: no more aligned rows, but more often a site plan based on urban composition.

The housing concepts adopted are numerous: apartments, semi-detached, villas. Apartment buildings could be low-rise — six storeys without elevator — or high-rise buildings, 35 storeys or more. Apartments could be on one floor or double-decked, built into a residential complex or independent. Villas could be in row or independent. Semi-detached houses could have two storeys, three storeys or more, or even two semi-detached houses one upon the other. A combination of all of the above is possible. The same building could have semi-detached house in the first two storeys and apartments in the upper storeys. One complex could have different kinds of styles: apartments — low and high-rise buildings — semi-detached houses and villas.

In the midst of such a huge differentiation and through such different social and political periods, we can find some constant elements. These constant elements, even transformed, have bridged the political and social periods, providing a connection between the past and the present day.

This guide will mainly consider the progressive transformation from Chinese tradition to modern styles and what could be considered the elements that remained constant through the process. The guide will consider the mixture between Chinese and Western concepts and elements.

This guide will focus on the concepts and architectural elements. It must largely ignore social issues. Buildings illustrated are examples of different concepts. There are many other buildings in the city similar to those illustrated.

Architectural, Urban and Symbolic Elements

Some elements — coming from Chinese tradition — are determinant. They are symbolic elements, which have acquired architectural and urban features. Their style shifted with the change in historical periods, but they remained constant elements. We could say that they are the connection between past and present. They are also the connection between the great transformation from the Chinese traditional concept to the Western/international modern concept.

These elements could be recognized in the following: the perimeter fence with one or two entrances/gates; the hierarchy of space; the south/north axis and the site plan. These elements can be of different styles, depending on historical periods and owners' taste.

These elements together create the characteristic residential housing scheme: the complex or compound or estate. This scheme comes from the Chinese tradition.

■ *Perimetric fence and gates.* The outer wall is a fundamental architectural element in China's construction culture. A wall surrounds all Chinese architectural complexes — with one or at most two entrances — the Imperial Palaces, the temples and residential areas. The entrances become architectural elements too, as do the gates.

■ *Spaces' hierarchy.* This also comes from Chinese tradition. There are different "steps" or "passages" from the public space to the private space: from the city to the family home. Each passage has an entrance. Each passage is an open area, a lane or a courtyard. The passages are: from the road to the central lane, the alley, the house courtyard and the internal rooms.

- *Mono-axis (south/north axis)*. The traditional Chinese layout for houses, temples and Imperial Palaces is always based on one axis (south/north) with perfect geometry and symmetry (south/north, east/west). The orientation and position of buildings follow this rule. The main facade always faces southward. This rule, chiefly dictated by climatic factors, has held well throughout China during every age.

- *Central lane, perpendicular alleys and series in row*. From the south entrance, the central lane crosses the whole area (the central axis). Perpendicular alleys lead to each dwelling. Alleys and buildings are aligned in rows on the east/west direction.

- *Complexes, compounds and villages*. Each residential area is like a small village inside the city. Each complex — surrounded by a wall with two entrances (usually south and north), constituted by different typologies, equipped with public facilities such as shops, schools, green areas, children's playgrounds — becomes an "enclave". These villages combined make up the city.

- *Styles*. Due to these concepts the architectural elements can be "covered" in different styles. The style chosen depends on the historical period, on the owners' and architects' taste and even on market requirements.

- *Facade*. The main axis is the south/north one both for the layout and the entrance direction, the principal — and unique — perception view is from south. Also most important is that the southward facade should face the garden. This comes from Chinese tradition, where the architecture perception is mainly from only one point: the south (a static layout).

- *Mono-axis, Style and Facade*. These elements joined together make a bi-dimensional architecture. Style and facade acquire an independent significance from the building itself (and from the internal space). There is a dichotomy between one another. Style is the exterior covering. The viewpoint from the south is the only one that is significant. The southern facade is the building's appearance. All of this is much more evident in private residences and villas, but is also visible in condominium buildings as well.

We could add another architectural element: the balcony. In Shanghai it appeared during the 1930s — or earlier — in the apartment blocks and some Longtang compounds. Nowadays the balcony is present in all residential buildings throughout the city. The balcony is the place people can watch the world outside and at the same time be seen by others (the intermediate zone between interior and exterior). In Europe, kings, Popes and common people have made use of the balcony throughout the ages.

Shanghai Residential Buildings

▲
Shu Yin Lou Gate

Shanghai Residential Buildings

▲ ◄ **Longtang Gates (1920s~1930s)**

▲ **Modern Gates (1990s)**

Shanghai Residential Buildings

Gates

▲ **Longtang Gates** (1910s~1920s)

▼▲ **Modern Gates** (1990s)

17

Shanghai Residential Buildings

Fences

▲ **Plastered Wall**

▲ **Traditional Bamboo Fence (Half Brick Wall)**

▲ **Modern Iron Fence**

▲ **Modern Iron Fence**

Shanghai Residential Buildings

◀▼ **Traditional Bamboo Fence**

▼ **Traditional Bamboo Fence**

*S*hanghai Residential Buildings

Central Lanes

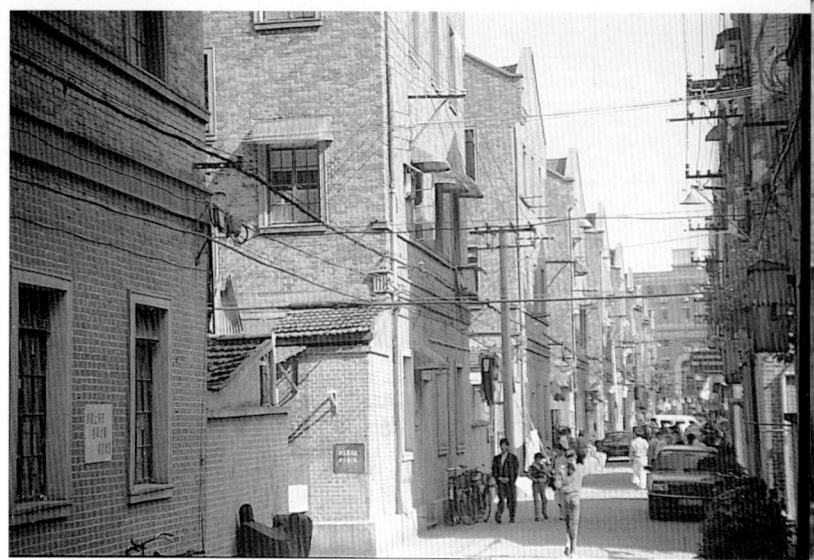

▲ 1920s

▲ 1950s

▲ 1930s

▲ 1930s

Shanghai Residential Buildings

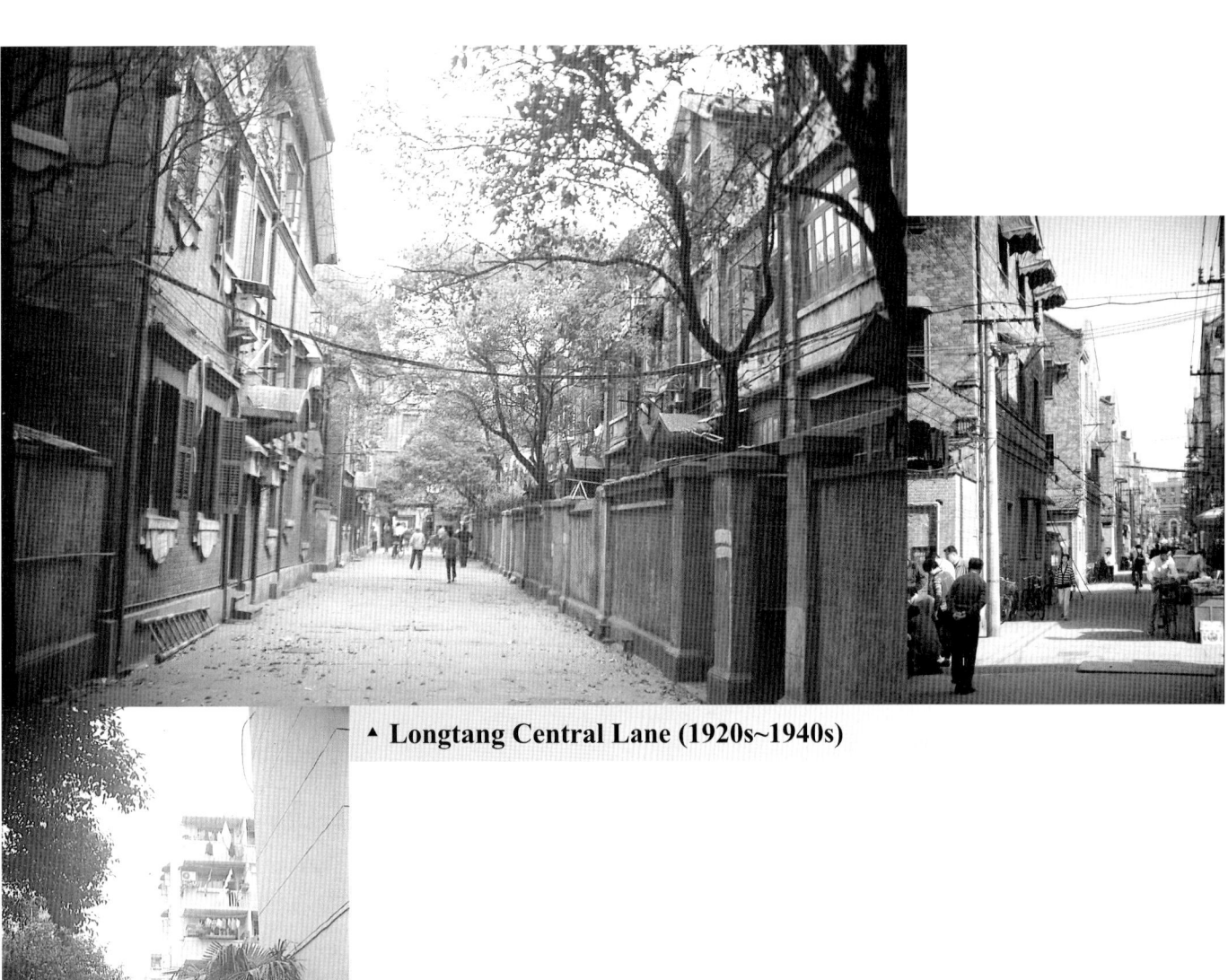

▲ Longtang Central Lane (1920s~1940s)

▲ Central Lane (1980s)

$\mathcal{S}$hanghai Residential Buildings   Series

▲ **Longtang (1930s)**

▲ **Modern Housing (1980s)**

▲ **Modern Housing (1980s)**   ▲ **Modern Housing Compound (1990s)**

Shanghai Residential Buildings

▲ **Modern Housing (1970s)**

Longtang (1930s) ▲▶

23

Shanghai Residential Buildings

▲ 1930s

▲ 1990s

▲ 1990s

▲ 1980s

Facade

South Facade

Shanghai Residential Buildings

▲ 1980s

North Facade

▲ 1980s

▲ 1930s

▲ 1990s

*S*hanghai Residential Buildings

▲ **Modern Style (1990s)**

▲ **Alsatian Style (1930s)**

▲ **Spanish Mediterranean (1990s)**

Styles

▲ **Arab Style (1920s)**

▲ **Mixed Chinese/Western (1930s)**

▲ **International Style (1990s)**

*S*hanghai Residential Buildings

27

Shanghai Residential Buildings

1 SHU YIN LOU RESIDENCE
书隐楼
77, Tiandeng Long
Huangpu District (formerly Nanshi District)
黄埔区（原南市区）巡道街天灯弄 77 号
18th century (1736-1796), Qing Dynasty

Historical Residence

This is the only remaining historical Chinese house in Shanghai (with the exception of the houses in YuYuan Gardens). It was built during the Qing Dynasty in the 18th century, and though nearly completely abandoned it is still there. Three courtyards and residential rooms, arranged on the south/north axis, constitute the house in a compact layout. A high brick wall (12 meters) surrounds the wooden structure rooms. (Sketch in Appendix 1)

28

Shanghai Residential Buildings

Shanghai Residential Buildings

30

Shanghai Residential Buildings

Progressive Transformation

No. 2
Residence in Pudong Lujiazui; 1927
Chinese traditional house with Western influence

No. 3-5
Independent residences;
Houses with Chinese and Western elements

No. 6-13
Shikumen Longtang; 1910s — 1920s
Residential compound with Chinese and Western elements

No. 14-18
Longtang; terraced
Residential compound with Chinese and Western elements

No. 19-26
Longtang; terraced, semi-detached, small detached and apartments
Residential compound with Chinese and Western elements

No. 27-29
Blocks of apartment buildings and semi-detached houses; 1930s
Western type with some Chinese elements

No. 30-32
Individual apartment buildings; 1930s
Western type and Western style

No. 33-36
Small detached; 1930s
Western type in a Chinese Layout; Western styles

No. 37-40
Independent residences; 1920s—1930s
Western type in Chinese layout; Western style

No. 41
Independent residence; 1930s
Western type in Chinese/Western style

No. 42-47
Villages and compound; low-rise and high-rise apartment buildings; 1950s-1980s
Residential compound with Chinese and Western elements

No. 48-54
Modern compounds; low-rise/high-rise apartment buildings, villas; 1990s
Residential compound with Chinese and international elements

No. 55-57
Independent apartment buildings; 1990s
International type and styles

No. 58-59
Modern villas in row; 1990s
Western type in a Chinese layout, Western styles

No. 60
New modern compounds; low-rise/high-rise apartment buildings, villas; late 1990s

Shanghai Residential Buildings

2 This is a modern example of a traditional Chinese house. Built in 1927, as in the Longtang houses both layout and architectural details are influenced by Western concepts. The traditional horizontal expansion has a compact layout even if not as compressed as the Longtang houses. Nowadays it is used as the Urban Plan Museum of Pudong Lujiazui New Financial Area.

Progressive Transformation

RESIDENCE IN PUDONG LUJIAZUI
陈桂春住宅
160, Lujiazui Lu
Pudong District
浦东陆家嘴路 160 号
1927

*S*hanghai Residential Buildings

An example of transition from the Chinese tradition to the Longtang houses. Two storeys, central courtyard, south direction. Compressed layout as in Longtang houses but wider courtyard surrounded by a portico on both storeys.

3

INDEPENDENT RESIDENCE
住宅
146, Jianguo Xi Lu
Luwan District
卢湾区建国西路 146 号

Shanghai Residential Buildings

SHIKUMEN
石库门

151/155/157, Houjia Lu
Huangpu District
(formerly Nanshi District)
黄浦区（原南市区）
候家路 151,155,157 号

4

Three houses united in a single block. One with three storeys and an internal yard, the other two with two floors and double yards facing the street (but not southwards) separated by a high wall. Black facebricks and recurrences of red bricks.

35

SHIKUMEN
石库门
175/179, Jin Jia Fang Lu
Huangpu District
(formerly Nanshi District)
黄浦区（原南市区）
金家坊路 175, 179 号

5

Two dwellings aligned with the street, facing south. Two floors, single internal yard, rooms along the sides of the yard, high wall separating the yard from the lane and front door with cornice. Black facebricks and recurrences of red bricks. Different architectural details for the two dwellings.

Typical example of the earliest type Longtang Shikumen. Single or shared yards. Black facebricks and recurrences in red bricks. Door cornices in gray concrete.

6

SHIKUMEN
石库门
Lane 136, Xiamen Lu
Huangpu District
黄浦区厦门路 136 弄

*S*hanghai Residential Buildings

7 This is one of the oldest blocks in existence: 1907. The typology is a single yard (with rooms along the sides) or two yards (separated by wall). Dense urban layout, with internal lanes and narrow alleys. The architecture is extremely simple, lacking in detail. Plastered walls.

HONG DE LI
洪德里
Lane 756, Beijing Dong Lu
Huangpu District
黄浦区北京东路 756 弄

Shanghai Residential Buildings

8

Large block of early Longtang Shikumen type. Single or shared yards, two or three floors. Black facebricks. Great attention to architectural details (cornices of doors and windows, ridge lines).

BAO KANG LI
保康里
Lane 803, Beijing Dong Lu
Huangpu District
黄浦区北京东路803弄

Shanghai Residential Buildings

9

Large and important block of early Longtang Shikumen type. Single yards, two storeys. Outside walls in red facebricks or plaster. Cornices of doors in facebricks. Wider central lane and side lanes.

KANG FU LI
康福里
Lane 906, Xinzha Lu
Jing'an District
静安区新闸路906弄

*S*hanghai Residential Buildings

SHIKUMEN
石库门
Lane 481, Taixing Lu
Jing'an District
静安区泰兴路 481 弄

10

Large and important block of early Longtang Shikumen type. Single or double yards or terraced type. Two storeys. Outside walls in black facebricks and recurrences in red bricks. Great wealth and variety of architectural details: cornices, string-course, ridge lines (in stone or facebricks).

41

Shanghai Residential Buildings

Shikumen Longtang type renovated in 1980s with internal facilities such as bathroom and kitchen added.

11

SHIKUMEN LONGTANG
里弄住宅
Lane 303, Penglai Lu
Huangpu District
(formerly Nanshi District)
黄埔区（原南市区）蓬莱路303弄
1910s-1920s

Shanghai Residential Buildings

12

SHIKUMEN
石库门
Lane 590-40/56, Weihai Lu
Jing'an District
静安区威海路 590 弄 40-56 号

Block of early Shikumen Longtang houses with specific aspects. The lanes separate nine very compact sub-units each taking on the appearance of a fortress, with internal alleys leading to single dwellings. Single yards. Two floors. Outside walls in black facebricks and recurrences in red bricks. Great wealth and variety of architectural details: cornices, string-course, ridge lines (in stone or facebricks).

43

*S*hanghai Residential Buildings

CITE BOURGOGNE
步高里

Jianguo Xi Lu (corner Shaanxi Nan Lu)
Luwan District
卢湾区建国西路（陕西南路路口）
1930s

13

An important block of Shikumen Longtang type houses. The gates opening to two city roads have strong architectural features.

44

Shanghai Residential Buildings

JIAN YE LI
建业里

Lane 440, Jianguo Xi Lu
Xuhui District
徐汇区建国西路 440 弄

14

Terraced block, with yards divided by high walls. Constructed in 1920. Very compact with narrow lanes and alleys. Two floors plus attic with dormer windows. Plain architectural details. Red facebricks. Protected as part of architectural heritage.

HUAIHAI TERRACE
淮海坊

Lane 899-927, Huaihai Zhong Lu
Luwan District
卢湾区淮海中路 899-927 弄

15 Large block and typical example of terraced Longtang housing. Year of construction: 1927. Three storeys, yard divided by walls (lower wall type). Compact south side with large windows, north split up in terms of volume by the alternation of solid and empty spaces (kitchens and rooms above, enclosures and terraces). Facebricks.

Shanghai Residential Buildings

16

BAO DE LI

褒德里

Lane 142, Wuyuan Lu
Xuhui District

徐汇区五原路 142 弄

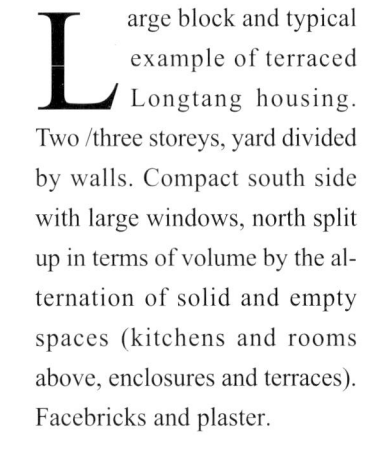

Large block and typical example of terraced Longtang housing. Two /three storeys, yard divided by walls. Compact south side with large windows, north split up in terms of volume by the alternation of solid and empty spaces (kitchens and rooms above, enclosures and terraces). Facebricks and plaster.

JING'AN ESTATE
静安别墅
Lane 1025, Nanjing Xi Lu
Jing'an District
静安区南京西路 1025 弄

17

Large block and typical example of terraced Longtang housing. Three storeys, yard (garden type) divided by walls (lower wall type). Western renaissance-like architectural details (balconies with columns and spiral corbels, Serlian-type windows). Facebricks. Protected as part of architectural heritage.

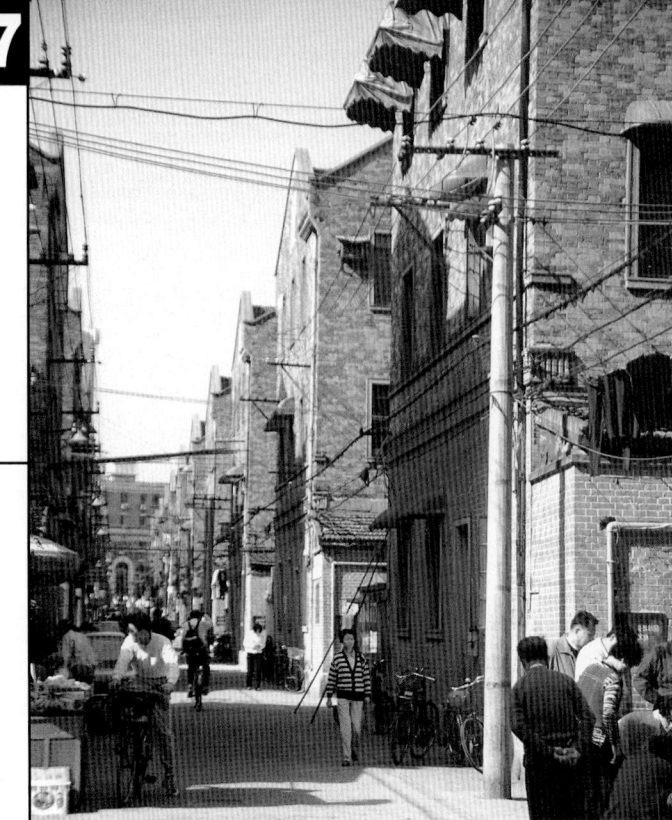

Shanghai Residential Buildings

18

Typical terraced housing with small front gardens. Year of construction: 1925. Their classification in the Longtang typology is due to their being united in a single block and to their perfect southward orientation. Two storeys. Architectural style: European Alpine. Protected as part of architectural heritage.

VERDUN GARDEN
凡尔登花园
Lane 39, Shaanxi Nan Lu
Luwan District
卢湾区陕西南路 39 弄

49

*S*hanghai Residential Buildings

19

Terraced housing with small gardens divided by fencing. The rows of buildings are not linked by a central lane but a city street. Two storeys. Architectural style: Spanish-Mediterranean.

RUI ZHI CUN
瑞之村
Lane 148, Jiaozhou Lu
Jing'an District
静安区胶州路 148 弄

Shanghai Residential Buildings

FUXING FANG
复兴坊
Lane 553, Fuxing Zhong Lu
Luwan District
卢湾区复兴中路553弄

20

Block containing different typologies: terraced, small detached, apartments. Three and five floors. Dwellings are not all oriented southwards. Facebricks, pitch roofs and wooden rafters below the pitch.

*S*hanghai Residential Buildings

21

Large block consisting of two parts. One part has three-storey buildings in a row, with four apartments per floor: very simple architecture. The second part consists of two-storey semi-detached houses, with small front garden: Spanish/Chinese architectural style. Year of construction: 1936.

YONGJIA TERRACE
永嘉新村

Lane 580, Yongjia Lu
Xuhui District
徐汇区永嘉路 580 弄

*S*hanghai Residential Buildings

Large block consisting of terraced housing (two storeys), semi-detached houses (two floors) in rows and a three-storey apartment building. Perfect southward alignment and orientation. Extensive green areas. Architectural style: Spanish Mediterranean.

TAIYUAN XIN CUN
太原新村
Lane 45, Taiyuan Lu
Xuhui District
徐汇区太原路 45 弄

22

*S*hanghai Residential Buildings

23

Block consisting of small detached houses (three storeys) in a row. Year of construction: 1938/39. Perfect southward alignment and orientation. Extensive green areas. Two architectural styles: Spanish Mediterranean and Rationalist.

SHANGFANG GARDEN
上方花园

Lane 1285, Huaihai Zhong Lu
Xuhui District
徐汇区淮海中路 1285 弄

Shanghai Residential Buildings

YUHUA XINCUN
玉华新村
Lane 182, Fumin Lu
Jing'an District
静安区富民路 182 弄

24

Block of three-storey semi-detached and terraced houses. In terms of volume, similar to the blocks in Lane 142, Wuyuan Lu and Lane 927, Huaihai Zhong Lu: compact south face, division of northern face, visible chimneys. Wright-style architecture.

25

Block consisting of two parts along an extensive central lane. One part consisting of four five-storey buildings in a row. Second part with eleven two-storey small detached houses with large front gardens. Architectural style: Spanish Mediterranean for detached houses and Rationalist for the high-rise buildings. Year of construction: 1933/34.

XINKANG GARDEN
新康花园

Lane 1360, Fuxing Zhong Lu
Lane 1273, Huaihai Zhong Lu
Xuhui District
徐汇区复兴中路 1360 弄
淮海中路 1273 弄

26

Block consisting of sixteen four-storey buildings in rows, with four apartments per floor. Green areas. Jutting pitch roofs, alternation of bricks and peel-effect plaster, polygonal bow windows in corners, chimneys visible. Period of construction: late 1920.

SHAAN NAN VILLAGE
陕南村
Lane 185, Shaanxi Nan Lu
Luwan District
卢湾区陕西南路 185 弄

*S*hanghai Residential Buildings

27

PUXI APTS.
浦西公寓
26, Zhapu Lu
Hongkou District
虹口区乍浦路 26 号

Multi-apartment Buildings And Semi-detached

1920s and 1930s

In the same compound three different typologies: semi-detached, Longtang and high-density apartment building. The semi-detached houses have interesting Western features. The nine storeys tall apartment building has Western features too: the layout follows the city's roads, the internal courtyard and the architecture style. One element comes from Chinese tradition — the entrance of the courtyard is on the south side from the internal lane.

*S*hanghai Residential Buildings

28 PARK APTS.
派克公寓

455, Fuxing Zhong Lu
Luwan District
卢湾区复兴中路 455 号

This multi-apartment building has both features from the West and China. The north facade follows the city's road. The "U" shape large courtyard is open to south.

EMBANKMENT BUILDING
河滨大楼

310-434, Bei Suzhou Lu
Hongkou District
虹口区北苏州路 310-434 号

A large multi-apartment building situated on the northern bank of the river Suzhou, basically looking southwards. Three floors and the roof terrace were added in the 1950s above the original eight storeys.

29

59

TAIXING APTS.
(FORMERLY MEDHURST APTS.)
泰兴公寓
（原麦特赫斯脱公寓）
934, Nanjing Xi Lu
Jing'an District
静安区南京西路 934 号

30

32

NANCHANG APTS.
(FORMERLY ASTRID APTS.)
南昌大楼
（原阿斯屈米特公寓）
294-316, Nanchang Lu
Luwan District
卢湾区南昌路 294-316 号

Individual Apartment Buildings (Western Type) 1930s

These three individual apartment buildings have only Western features in their type and style. In these cases the differences between Western and Chinese tradition are evident.

The apartment buildings have at least four or five storeys (in recent times more), two or three or more apartments for each storey, a courtyard in the center. The courtyard provides light and air for the internal rooms. Sometimes the courtyard leads to more stairs that divide the dwellings on the different storeys.

There are two other features in which the difference from the Chinese tradition is more evident.

Shanghai Residential Buildings

Usually the buildings follow and determine the city roads. This means that the block's area determines the buildings' layout, or, vice versa, the building determines the city road layout. There is a relation between the city layout and the building layout. On the other hand there is not a preference for the southward direction as in Chinese tradition, where there is no relation between the city layout and the building layout.

The second feature is the position of the main entrance. Usually in Western tradition the main entrance is directly on the city road. The hierarchy that orders the Chinese residential area in progressive passages from the city road to the private dwellings is almost absent in the West.

31

CHANGDE APTS.
(FORMERLY EDDINGTON HOUSE)
常德公寓 （原爱林登公寓）
195, Changde Lu
Jing'an District
静安区常德路 195 号

*S*hanghai Residential Buildings

33

FORMER RESIDENCE OF SUN YAT-SEN
孙中山故居
7, Xiangshan Lu
Luwan District
卢湾区香山路 7 号

Small Detached Houses, 1930s

34

FORMER RESIDENCE OF SOONG CHING LING
宋庆龄故居
1843, Huaihai Zhong Lu
Xuhui District
徐汇区淮海中路 1843 号

Shanghai Residential Buildings

These villas and small detached residences are examples of houses found widely throughout the city: Western type and style in a Chinese layout (southward and garden on south side). Those illustrated were the residences of important leaders of modern China.

35

FORMER RESIDENCE OF ZHOU ENLAI
周恩来故居

70, Sinan Lu
Luwan District
卢湾区思南路 70 号

36

FORMER RESIDENCE OF ZHANG XUE LIANG (NOW CONSULATE OF THE NETHERLANDS)
张学良故居

1, Gaolan Lu
Luwan District
卢湾区皋兰路 1 号（现荷兰领事馆）

63

37
CHILDREN'S PALACE (FORMERLY KADOORIE HOUSE)
上海市少年宫
（原嘉道理住宅）
64, Yan'an Xi Lu
Jing'an District
静安区延安西路 64 号

38
XINGGUO HOUSE
兴国宾馆
72, Xingguo Lu
Changning District
长宁区兴国路 72 号

Villa/Residence Type 1920s-1930s

The independent residence — villa — is a typology imported from the West. These buildings are in Western styles (Neo-Renaissance, Norwegian or Alpine style, Rationalistic, Neo-classic or Colonial) but their layout is adapted to Chinese tradition. They have a southward direction, in some cases the main facade, in other cases the main entrance too. A garden on the south side is in front of the main facade. These buildings represent one solution of mixture architecture: a Chinese substance and a Western dress.

Shanghai Residential Buildings

39

FORMER MOLLER HOUSE
原马勒住宅
30, Shaanxi Nan Lu
Jing'an District
静安区陕西南路 30 号

40

FORMER D.V. WOO'S HOUSE
原吴同文住宅
333, Tongren Lu
Jing'an District
静安区铜仁路 333 号

65

*S*hanghai Residential Buildings

**RESIDENCE
(NOW USED AS OFFICES)**
住宅（现改作办公室）
200, Xinhua Lu
Changning District
长宁区新华路 200 号

Independent Residence 1930s

41

This building represents another solution of mixed architecture: almost diametrically opposite from the previous ones. The typology — villa — is imported from the West. The building's position in the land area follows Western concepts: in front of the gate from the city road. The style is a mixture of China and the West.

*S*hanghai Residential Buildings

CAOYANG NEW ESTATE
曹阳新村
Caoyang Lu
Putuo District
普陀区曹阳路

42

The first estate designed after 1949 by the government architectural institutes to solve the housing problems. Three or four storey buildings, wide green areas, sloping roof. In nearby areas there are housing complexes built in subsequent decades.

New Estate 1950s

67

Shanghai Residential Buildings

43 Six large apartment buildings thirteen storey each built in 1970s are in a row beside the city road facing south.

APARTMENT BUILDINGS
高层住宅群
Caoxi Bei Lu
Xuhui District
徐汇区漕溪北路

*S*hanghai Residential Buildings

New Estate 1980s

HUTAI NEW ESTATE
沪太新村

Hutai Lu
Putuo District
普陀区沪太路

44 One of the estates designed during the 1980s by a government architectural institute to solve the housing problem. They represent the typical modern residential areas: different typologies (low-rise and high-rise apt. buildings), public facilities inside, such as schools and green areas. Hutai New Estate can house about 60,000 inhabitants.

沪太新村居住小区规划设计图

*S*hanghai Residential Buildings

New Estate and Compound 1980s

45 | **XIANXIA NEW ESTATE**
仙霞新村
Xianxia Lu, Tianshan Lu
Changning District
长宁区天山路, 仙霞路

*S*hanghai Residential Buildings

46

One of the estates designed during the 1980s by government architectural institutes to solve housing problems and one compound that represents housing residential areas in the 1980s. Nearby there are previous housing complexes built in the 1950s.

▼ **Sketch Map of Furong Compound**

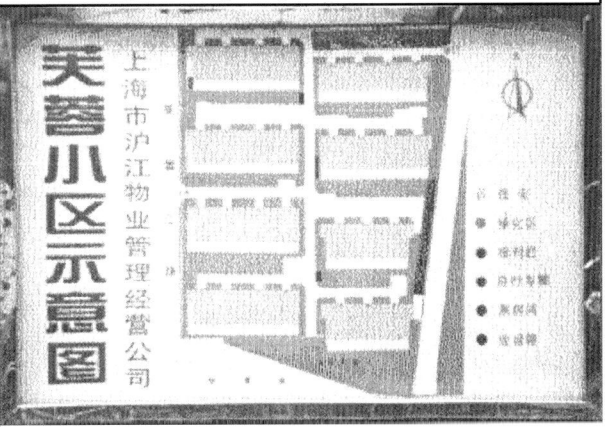

FURONG COMPOUND
芙蓉小区

Lane 103, Furongjiang Lu
Changning District
长宁区芙蓉江路 103 弄

71

*S*hanghai Residential Buildings

Two Compounds
1980s and late 1990s

47

HONGQIAO ESTATE
虹桥新村
Lane 377, Honggu Lu
Changning District
长宁区虹古路 377 弄

Sketch Map of Hongqiao Estate ▶

Shanghai Residential Buildings

PERFECT GARDEN
西郊华庭

Lane 1889, Hongqiao Lu
Changning District
长宁区虹桥路 1889 弄

48

These two neighboring compounds represent two periods — and two styles: one designed by government architectural institutes in the 1980s, the second by private investors in the late 1990s. Similar layout (buildings in row, southward direction), four or six storeys, semi-detached, double-deck and one floor apts., internal facilities and no elevator for both compounds.

*S*hanghai Residential Buildings

Modern Compounds; Low-rise/High-rise Apartment Buildings, Villas; Late 1990s

49

The following six compounds represent new residential house solutions by private investors both for architecture and urban layout. Multi - storey apartment buildings in row southward direction, a central lane, a common house and green areas in the middle are the features. Modern architecture.

GARDEN MUSEUM
西郊龙柏香榭苑
169, Qingshan Lu (corner Huanhua Lu)
Minhang District
闵行区青杉路 169 号（黄桦路路口）

50

TIME OF SPORT
韵动时代
Lane 462, Jinhui Lu,
Longbai Xincun
Minhang District
闵行区龙柏新村金汇路462弄

*S*hanghai Residential Buildings

51

TOMSON GARDEN
汤臣豪园
Lane 666, Long Dong Da Dao
Pudong District
浦东龙东大道 666 弄

76

Shanghai Residential Buildings

52

CENTURY GATE
世纪之门

Lane 1415, Jiangning Lu
Putuo District
普陀区江宁路1415弄

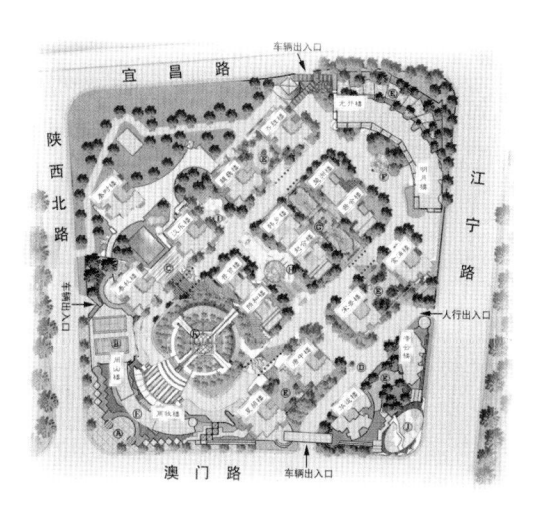

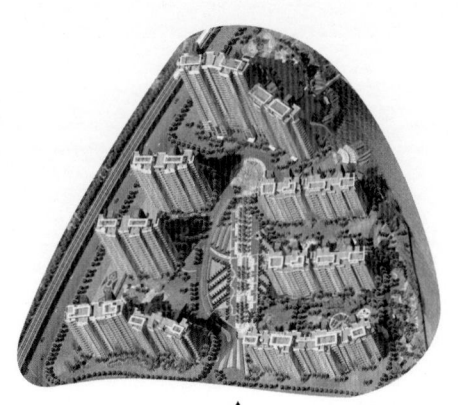

Shanghai Residential Buildings

Project Bird-eye View (first phase)

53

21ST CENTURY SEA SHORE PLAZA
21世纪海岸广场

Lane 1555, Kaixuan Bei Lu
Putuo District
普陀区凯旋北路1555弄

78

Shanghai Residential Buildings

Project Bird-eye View of Whole Complex
▼

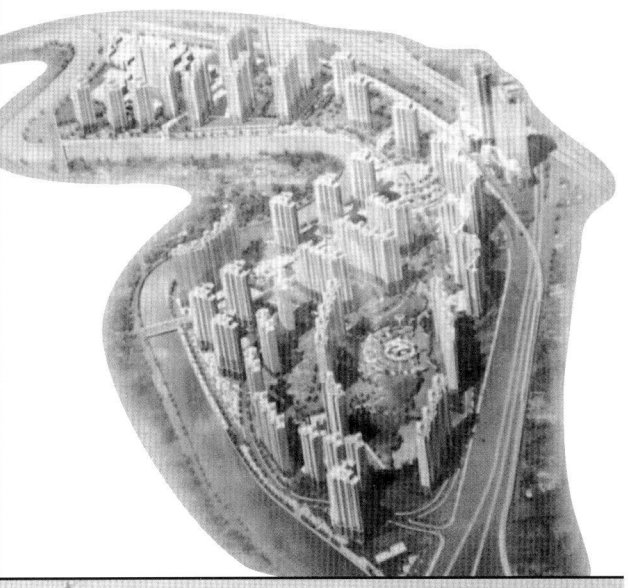

54

BRILLIANT CITY
中远两湾城
Zhongtan Lu
Putuo District
普陀区中潭路

79

Shanghai Residential Buildings

55

GEE HOUSE
芝大厦

41, Hengshan Lu
Xuhui District
徐汇区衡山路41号

Individual Apartment Buildings 1990s

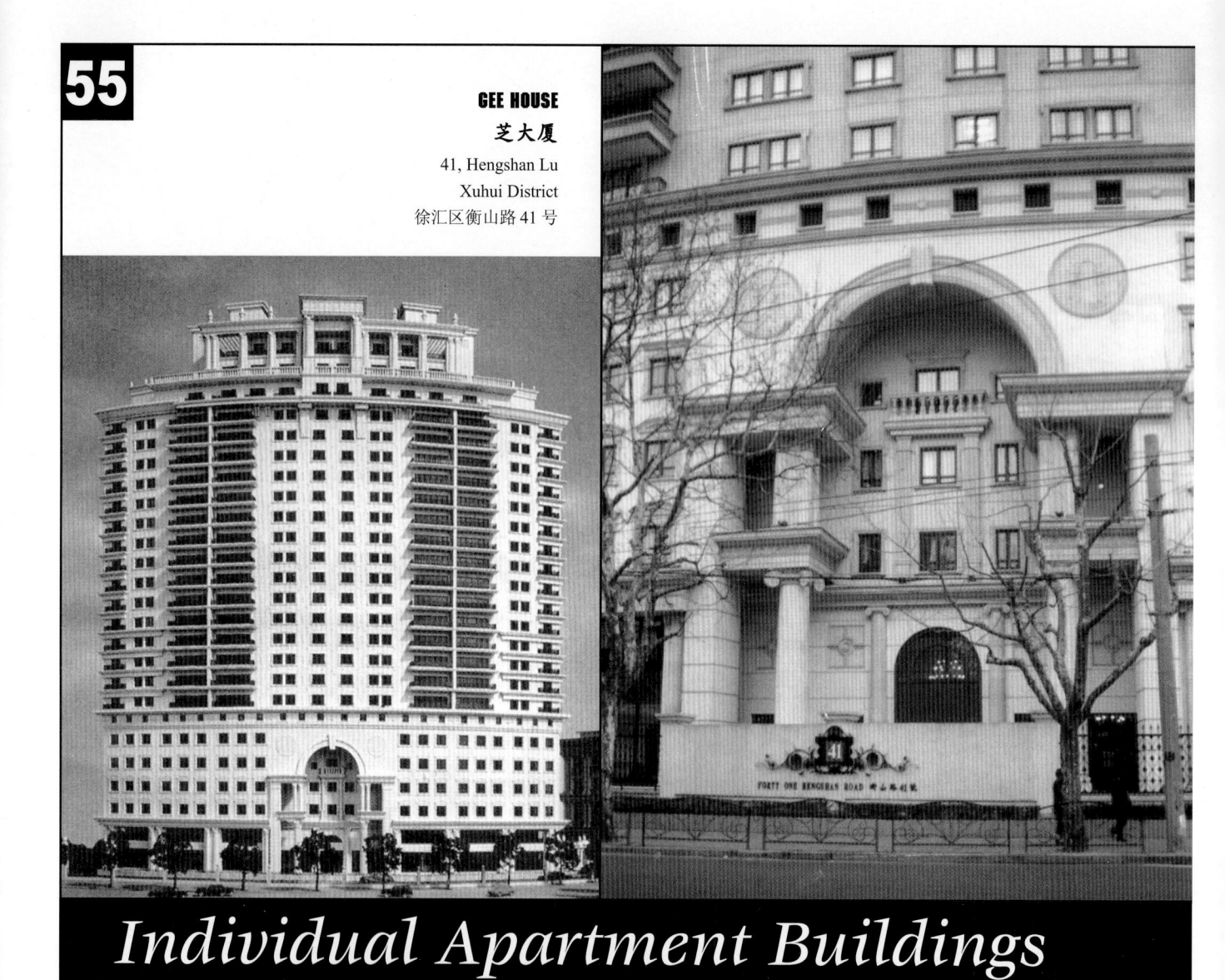

These three independent apartment buildings have similar features to those of the 1930s but with contemporary styles and modern facilities. All of the three buildings face the main street. The main door is directly on the city road. The Gee House has a symmetrical layout and curved facade in European style (Post Modern architecture). The Regent House is a high-rise building in International style and in a double symmetrical layout. The Chevalier Place follows the city roads' corner in an "L" shape layout.

*S*hanghai Residential Buildings

57

CHEVALIER PLACE
亦园

Wulumuqi Zhong Lu
Xuhui District
徐汇区乌鲁木齐中路

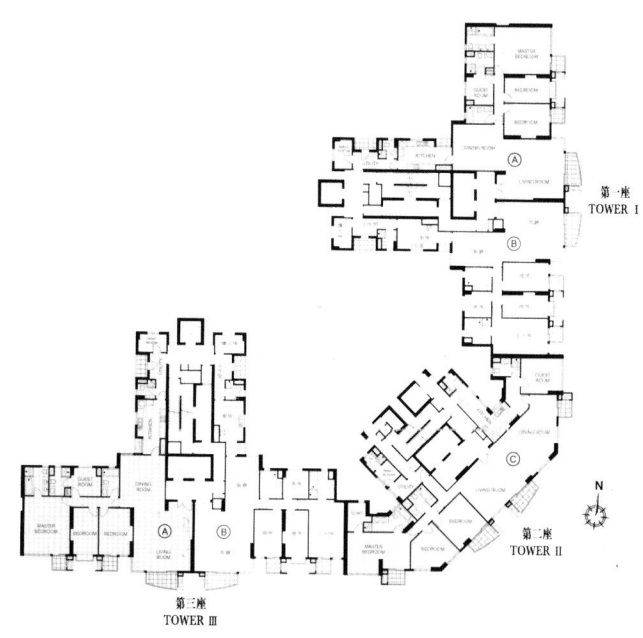

56

REGENT HOUSE
丽晶大厦

28, Xianxia Lu
Changning District
长宁区仙霞路28号

Shanghai Residential Buildings

Modern Villas In Row
Late 1990s

CONTEMPORARY VILLAS
当代艺墅

58

1801, Gudai Lu
Minhang District
闵行区顾戴路 1801 号

82

HONGQIAO GOLF VILLA
虹桥高尔夫别墅

Hongxu Lu
Minhang District
闵行区虹许路

59

These compounds of modern luxurious villas are both in the western area of Shanghai. Luxurious villa compounds are also in Pudong near the new Century Park. The villa compounds have big green areas and many common facilities (swimming pool, tennis court, gymnasium, etc.). The architecture is rich in details no matter the style. The dwellings have many internal facilities (kitchen, laundry room, servant room, bathroom, etc.). The layout comes from the Chinese tradition: the houses are arranged in rows usually facing south. In these cases could be two different solutions in the relation between the building position and the land. One is from Chinese tradition: the edifice is located on the north side of the land so that the garden is mostly on south side. The second is from Western tradition: the edifice's position is in the center of the land so that the garden has almost the same dimension on all sides. Nowadays the second one is more frequent (see the differences from the single residences in the 1930s; No. 33-40).

Shanghai Residential Buildings

(世茂滨江花园社区园林规划图)

New Modern Compounds
Late 1990s and Beginning of 21st Century

60

The new compounds along the Huangpu River follow new ideas for layout. The riverside view determines the buildings' position on the land. This means that the main facade is not facing south but towards the river. Two examples of the new trend: Yanlord Garden and Shimao Riviera. Yanlord Garden built in the late 1990s has a big green area in the middle: the buildings around the common space all have views of the Huangpu River. Shimao Riviera is under construction. The buildings have a "wave" shape layout following the river.

84

*S*hanghai Residential Buildings

Existing Buildings Roofed In Late 1990s

The Municipal Design Bureau has roofed many existing buildings with metal panels. Usually those buildings were built in the decades from the 1960s to 1980s with a terrace on the top. They are very simple both in architecture and facilities. The new roof solves two problems: better weatherproof solution (against heat, cold and rain) and a new skyline for the building itself and for the entire city.

85

Appendix 1
Layout Examples

Appendix 2
Housing and Symbols, Living Style in Shanghai

Appendix 1:
Layout Examples

In Appendix 1 there are some examples of dwelling's layout: from 1920s to the end of 1990s and beginning of the new century.

The historical Shu Yin Lou Residence (No. 1), built in the 18th century during the Qing Dynasty, is the cultural heritage in Shanghai. The house is one of the traditional Chinese dwelling's types. A high brick wall — without windows — surrounds the timber structure rooms. The rooms have big doors towards the internal courtyards. The main gate faces south. The layout is closed and centripetal.

The first modern example is the Residence in Pudong Lujiazui built in 1927 (No.2). This residence --- even if already influenced by the Western concepts --- is strong and deeply rooted in the Chinese tradition. It follows the south-north axis according to Chinese tradition. The house has its core in the central courtyard. The rooms --- and the corridors and the other small courtyard --- are arranged around the main central space: the open-air court. The rooms have big lattice windows towards the internal court. There are small windows on the perimetric walls. The habitation has a centripetal layout.

The latest example is the arrangement in the Regent Tower: a high-rise residential building built in 1997 (No.56). Each floor has four individual apartments in a double symmetric layout (left-right and front-rear). Each apartment occupies one corner of the plan (H shape). In the center there are the elevators, the stairs and other service rooms as the standard high-rise buildings' construction. Each apartment has big windows and balcony towards all directions (no matter south, north, front or rear). This layout has an opposite nature of the previous ones.

Between the two, there are the transformation and transition examples. Some of them have more Chinese elements. Some of them have more Western and international elements. No matter the quantity of dwellings or apartments in a single building, no matter the size, no matter the typology and no matter the style the transformation concerns first of all the dwelling's layout.

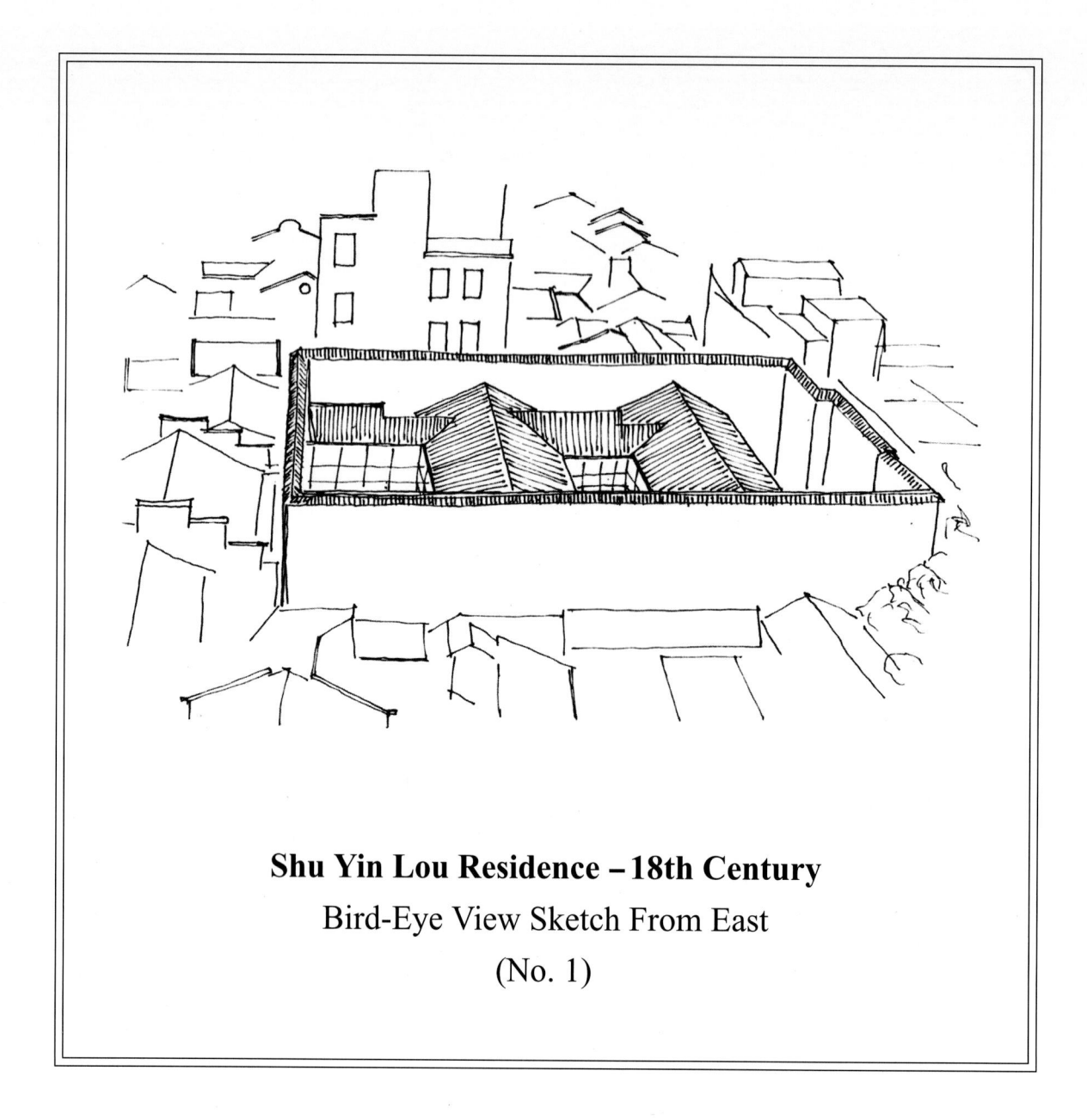

*S*hanghai Residential Buildings

Shu Yin Lou Residence – 18th Century
Bird-Eye View Sketch From East
(No. 1)

Residence in Pudong Lujiazui - 1927

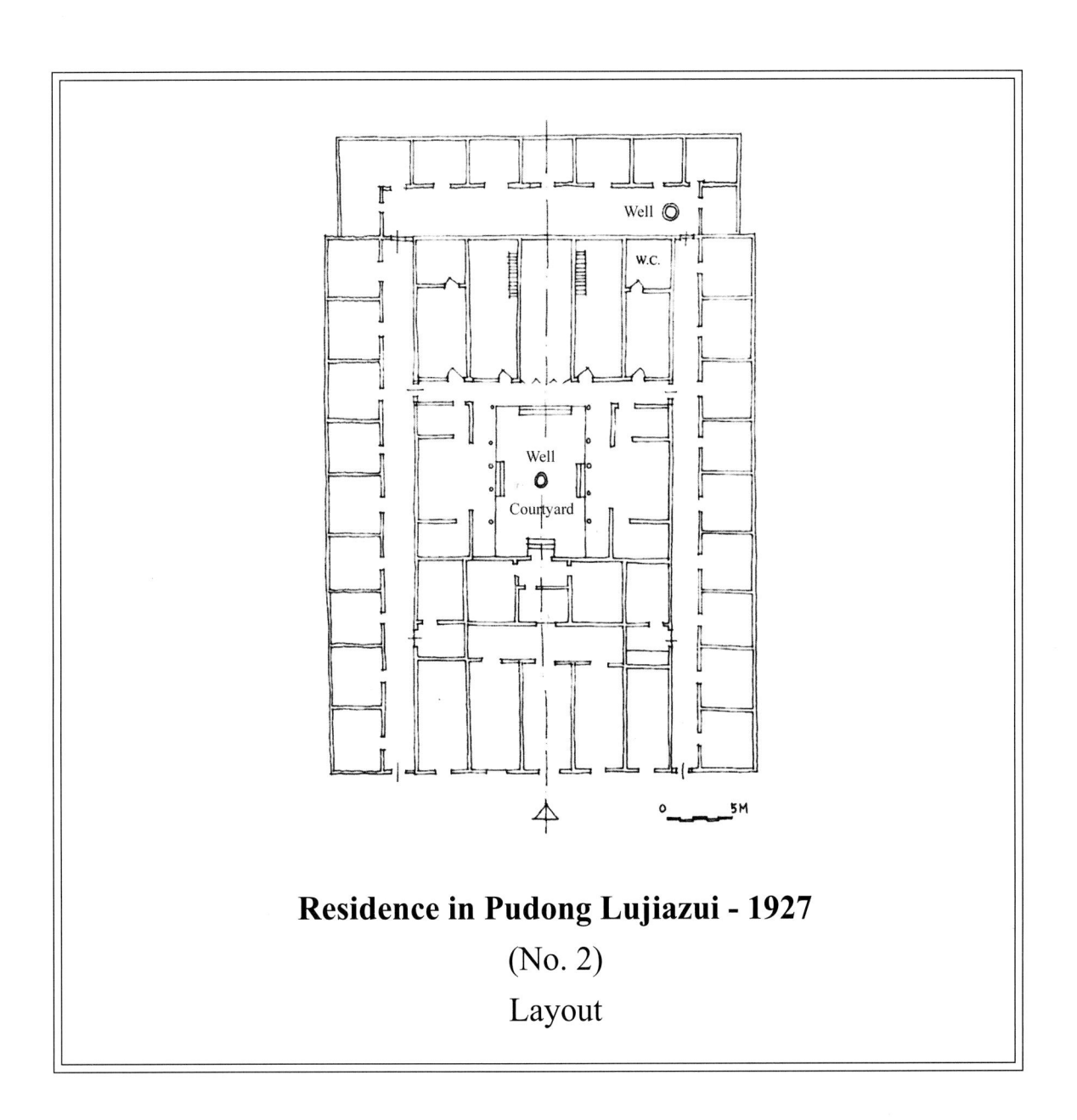

(No. 2)

Layout

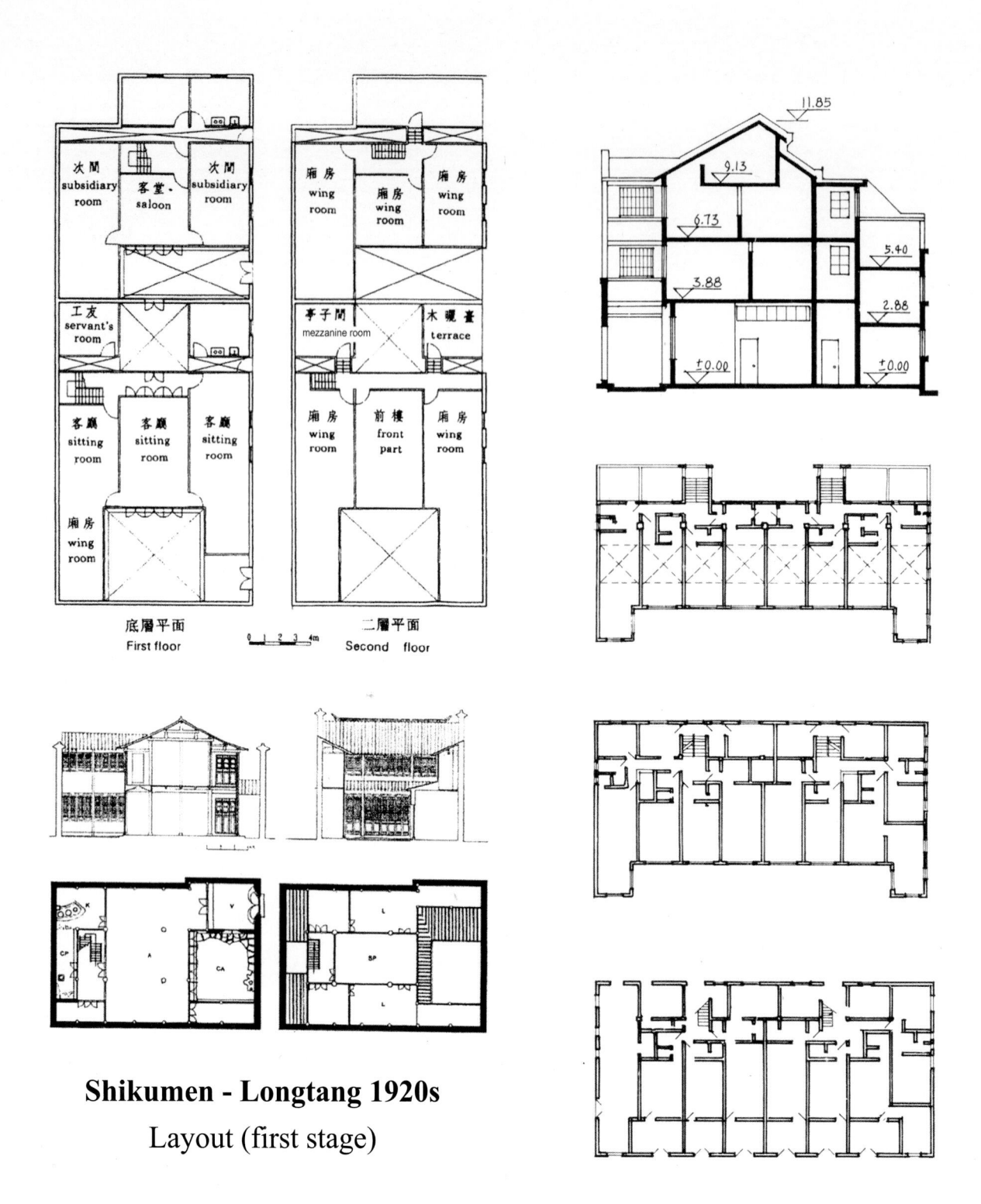

Shanghai Residential Buildings

次間 subsidiary room	客堂 saloon	次間 subsidiary room
工友 servant's room		
客廊 sitting room	客廊 sitting room	客廊 sitting room
廂房 wing room		

底層平面 First floor

廂房 wing room	廂房 wing room	廂房 wing room
亭子間 mezzanine room		木曬臺 terrace
廂房 wing room	前樓 front part	廂房 wing room

二層平面 Second floor

Shikumen - Longtang 1920s
Layout (first stage)

90

Shanghai Residential Buildings

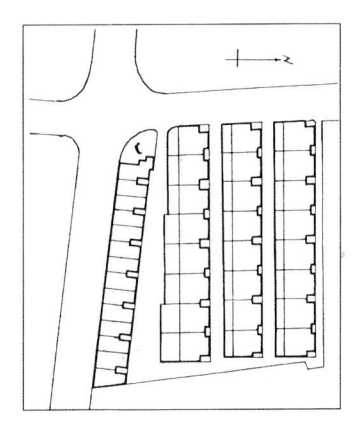

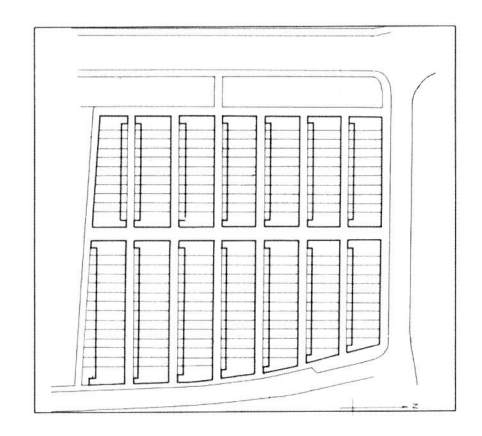

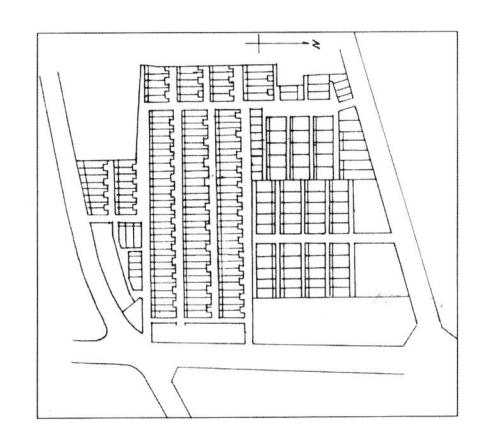

Longtang Site Plan

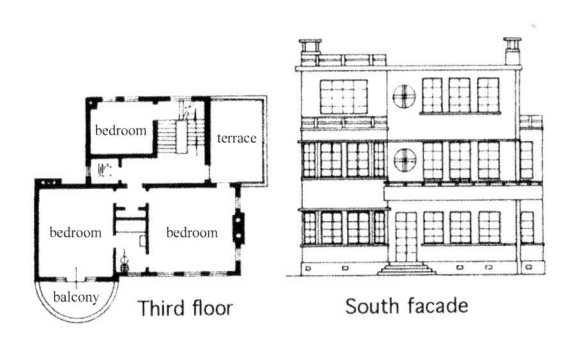

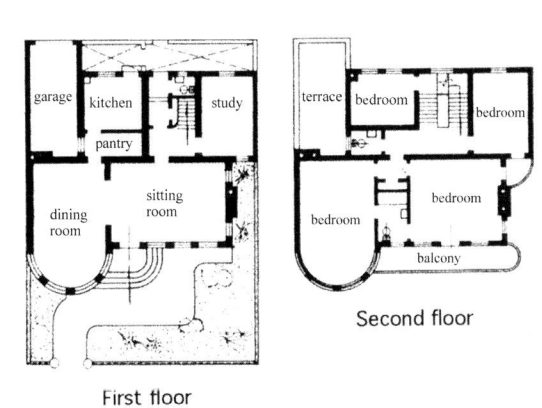

Shangfang Garden - 1930s
(No. 23)

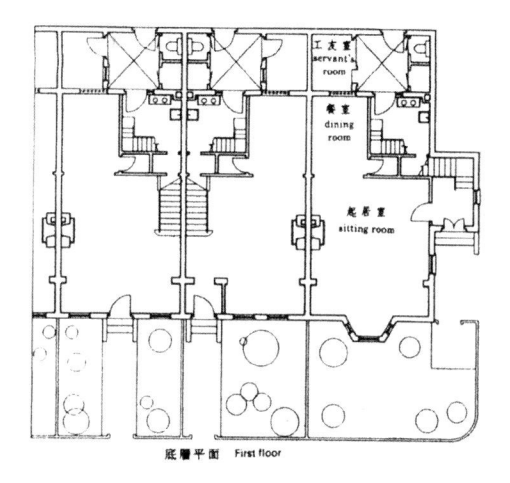

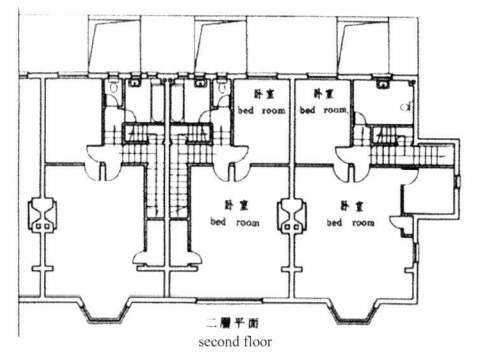

Verdun Garden - 1930s
(No. 18)

91

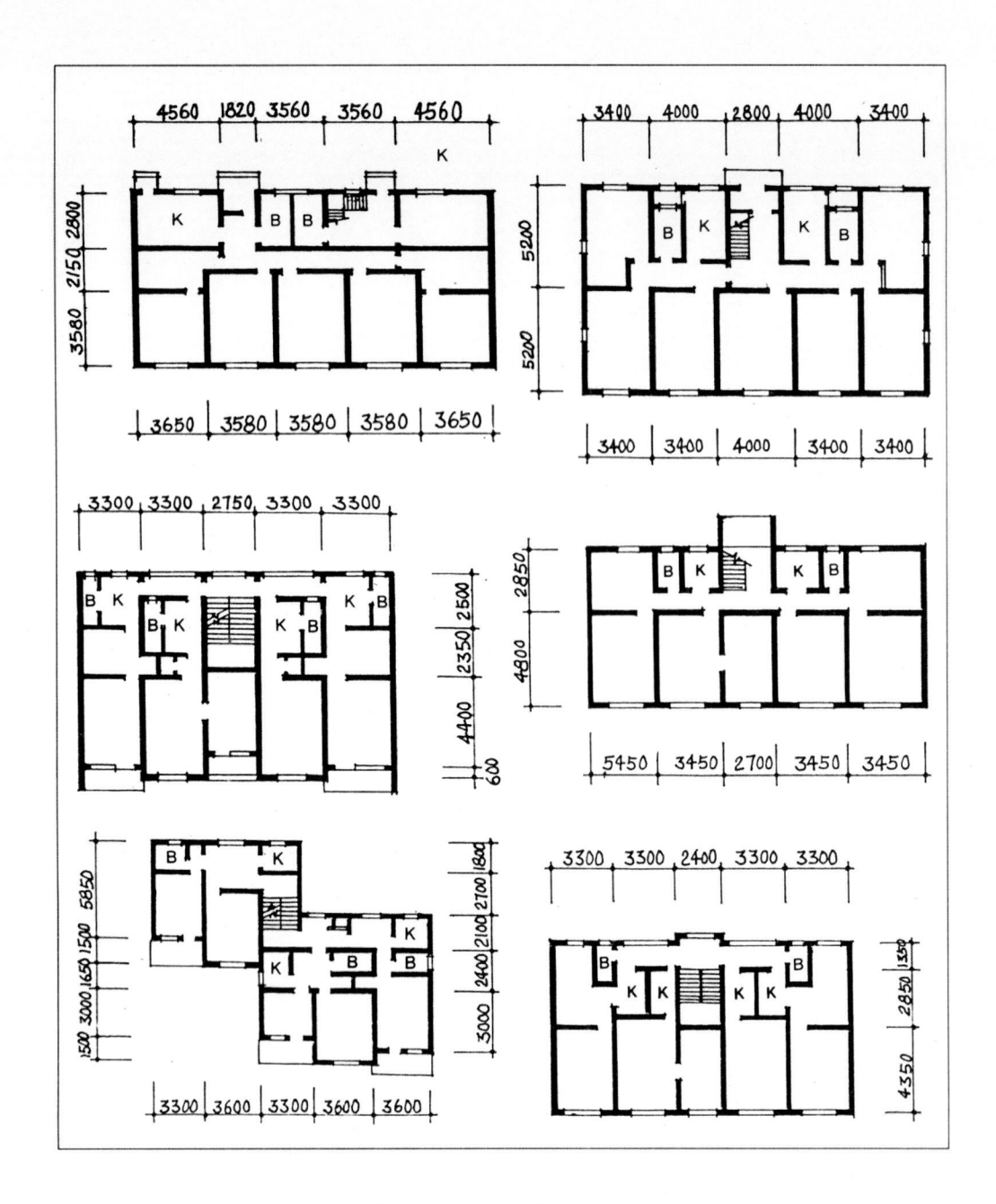

**Apartment Layout
From 1950s to 1980s
Examples**

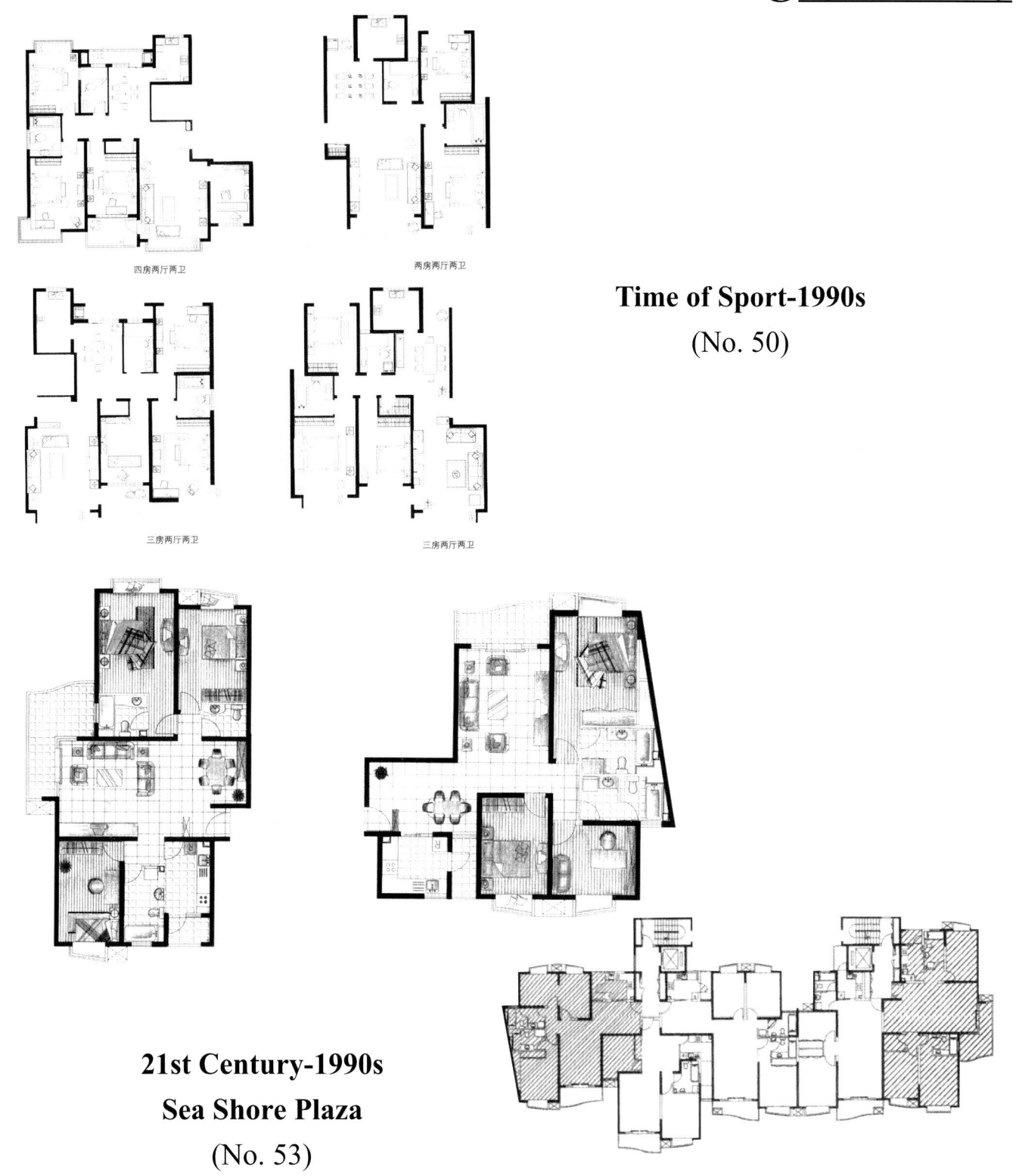

Shanghai Residential Buildings

四房两厅两卫　　　　　两房两厅两卫

Time of Sport-1990s

(No. 50)

三房两厅两卫　　　　　三房两厅两卫

**21st Century-1990s
Sea Shore Plaza**

(No. 53)

93

*S*hanghai Residential Buildings

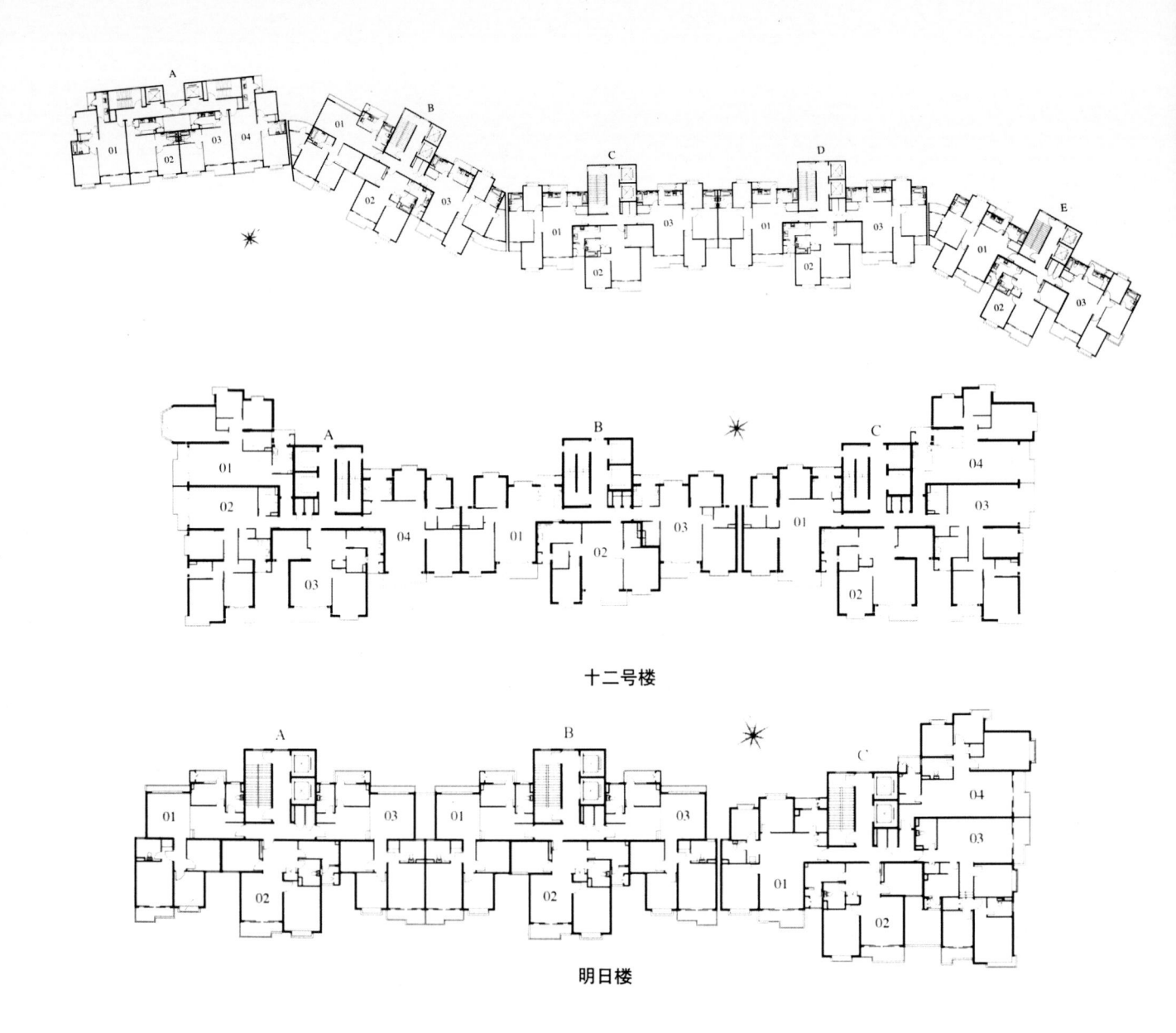

十二号楼

明日楼

Brilliant City - 1990s
(No. 54)

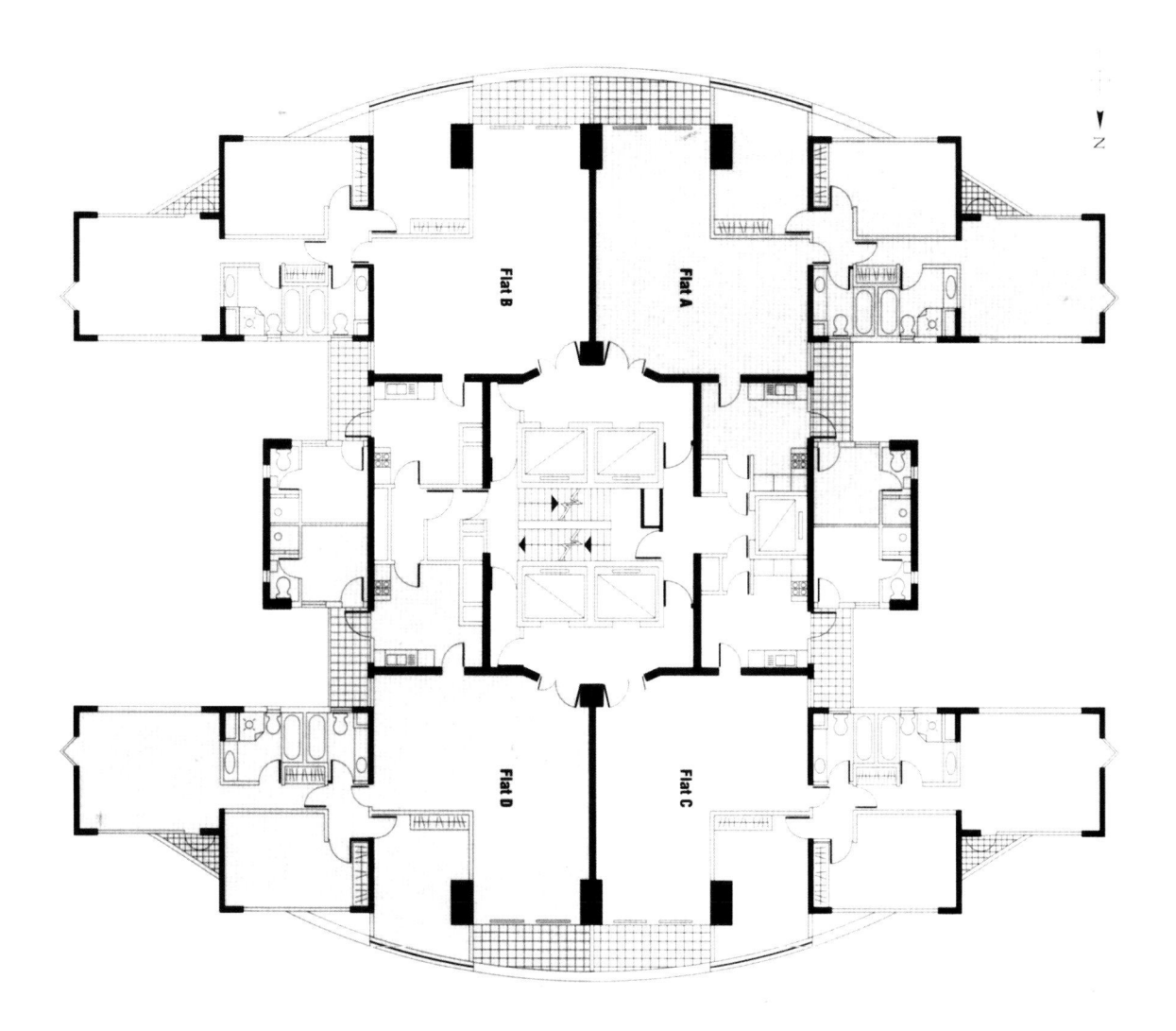

Regent Tower - 1997
Typical Floor
(No. 56)

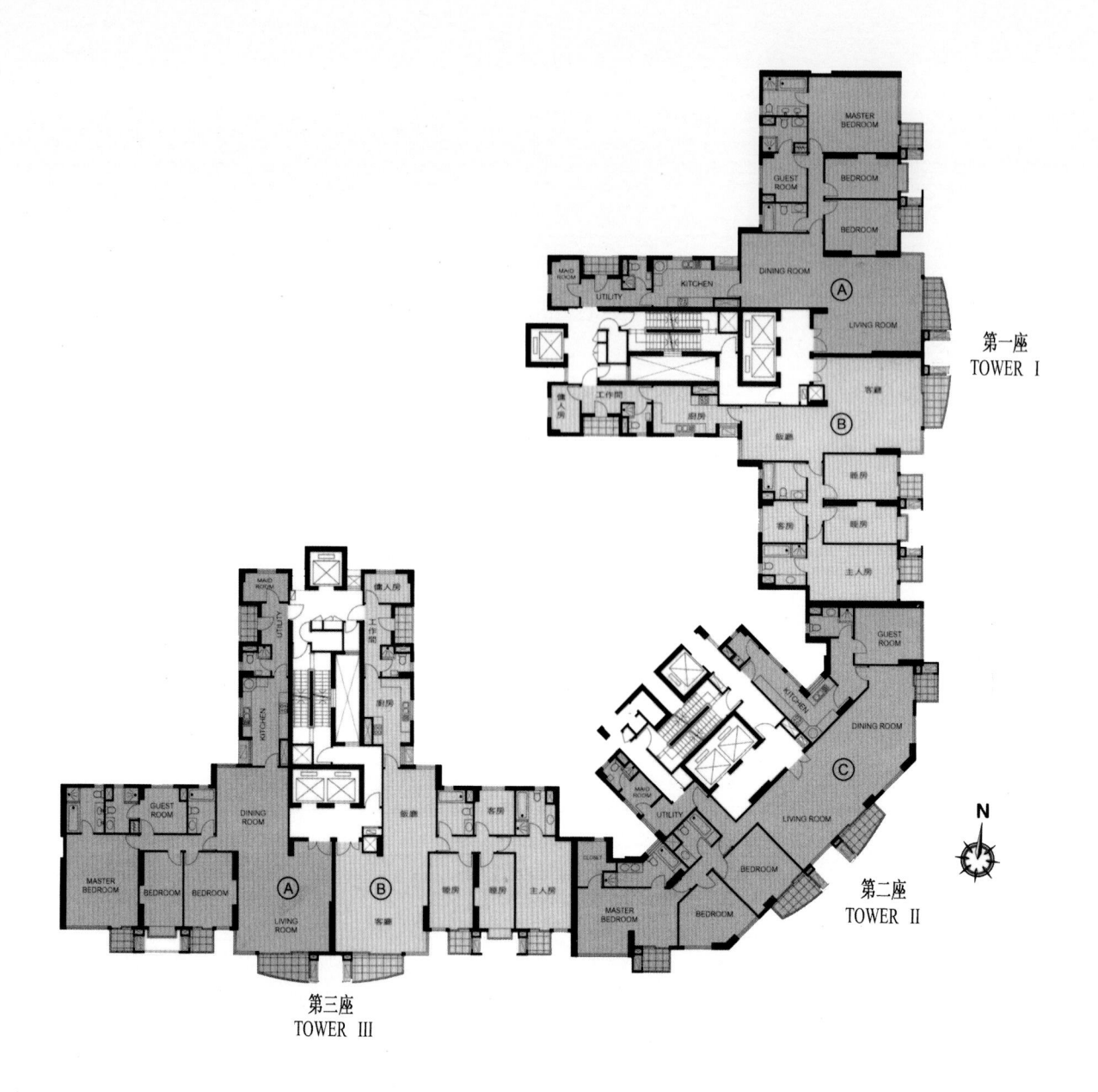

Chevalier Place - 1990s

(No. 57)

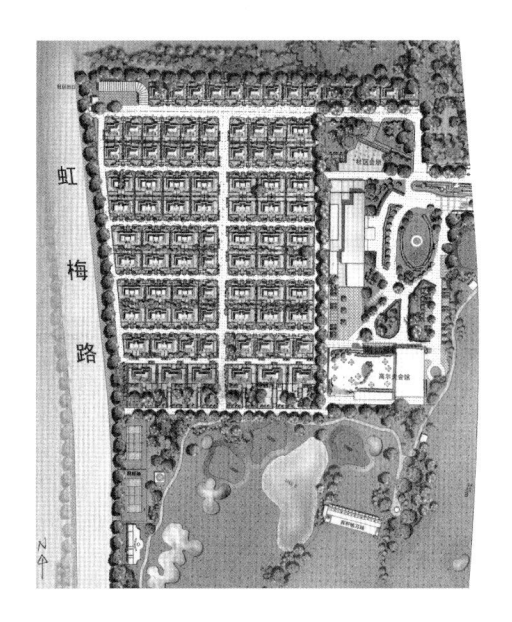

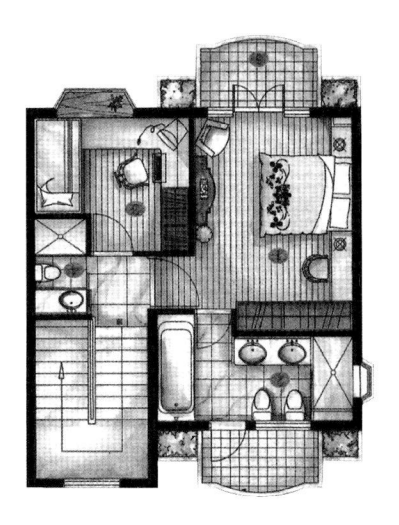

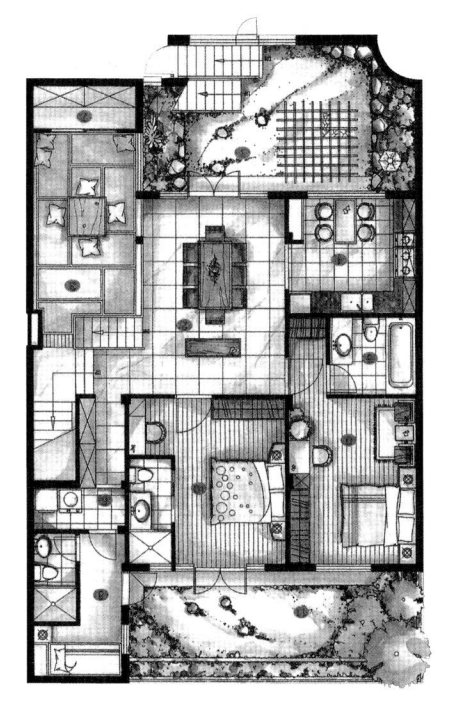

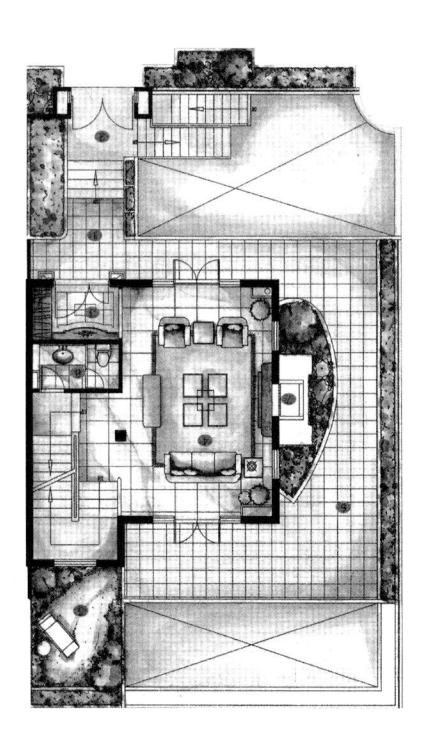

Hongqiao Golf Villa - 1990s

(No. 59)

Appendix 2:

Housing and Symbols, Living Styles in Shanghai

Since my first visit to Shanghai in April 1992 until 2002, I saw, visited, worked and lived in many houses throughout the city: apartments, villas and small detached houses, old and new, for Chinese and for foreigners, completed or under construction.

First of all, I noticed the Shanghai Longtang Houses as special buildings. Second, I noticed Western elements and Chinese elements — but it is better to call them "symbols" — around the city. Third, I noticed the transformation of housing during this decade. The relationship between construction solutions and lifestyles is evident in the residential areas.

In April 1992, I was hosted by my Chinese family's home in Jing'an District, just north of the Shanghai Center. It was a semi-detached house opening onto the street. It was French in style: three storeys, with brick walls, wooden floors and stairs, and a mansard roof. My host family lived on the third floor, under the roof: five people with less than 50 square meters of living space. They had a bathroom and a kitchen exclusively for themselves with the kitchen and bathroom sharing the same room: on the left side were the bathroom facilities (tube, basin and toilet), and on the right side, the kitchen counter with stove and basin. One door, one window. I slept in the so-called "tingzijian" room: on the mezzanine floor between the second and the third. A few years later it was demolished for a new high-rise building.

When I visited a relatives' home — a Longtang dwelling in Yangpu District — I immediately realized it as the most special house that I had ever seen, even if the complex as a whole lacked any interesting architectural features. At that time, they had no indoor bathroom. A communal toilet was located at the entrance of the complex. A few years later, my Chinese relatives installed a motor-driven sewage system. But many others still lack an indoor toilet.

In late 1992, my Chinese family moved from Jing'an District to Changning District, in the western suburbs of the city. The new apartment — located on the second floor of a fifteen-storey building built in the 1980s — had an indoor bathroom and kitchen in two separate rooms; southern exposure for the living room, one bedroom and a veranda. Its area was about 60 square meters for four persons.

During the 1990s, other relatives moved from a small house to a new and much bigger apartment in Xuhui District.

Later I lived in Honggu Road, in a modern lane residential area. Here I recognized the real living style of a Chinese compound or "village". The apartment was on the third floor, and the living room and the only bedroom were on the south side. There was a veranda on this side too. Bathroom, kitchen and stairs were on the north side. I noticed the big difference between the south facade — verandas and big windows — and the north facade — small windows for bathroom and stairs.

The building was on the third row in from the road so that there was no noise. The inner lanes had trees. Here the elder people would chat or play *majiong*. Children played. My daughter went to a kindergarten in a neighboring compound. Sometimes on the way she would stop and play with other children. At nine o'clock in the evening, someone walked around the whole compound ringing a hand-bell. This was the signal that the day was coming to a close, the night was coming and it was better to lock the doors.

I noticed the alignment of the buildings: one beside the other, one behind the other. The main rooms and verandas are always on the south facade, stairs and facilities rooms on the north side. Nothing, neither buildings nor lanes, was in a different position. This layout reminds me of the Terraccotta Warriors in Xi'an: one beside the other, one behind the other. They are all looking forward in the same direction.

When I restored the modern villa of a diplomatic family near Huaihai Road I noticed a similar layout in the villa compound. The same building is repeated five times, aligned in a row, very close to one another. On the south side is a small garden. I also noticed a similar layout in a golf resort on the outskirts of Shanghai where I restored villas. Eighty villas aligned in rows. Villas, Longtang houses, apartment buildings also have similar site plans.

The same building repeated many times — in a homogenous and uniform environment — brings peace to daily life. In the 1950s-1980s' developments, the predominant gray color enhances the peaceful environment too: gray plastered buildings and gray lane pavements. The gray color has a base in tradition. It comes from the Beijing hutong alleys where the houses were gray — both walls and roofs (in contrast the Imperial Palace was colorful: yellow roof, red wood).

The living style in Shanghainese compounds is completely different from what I was used to in Rome. Of course, the living style in the inner lanes reminds me of the small towns and ancient districts of big cities in Italy and Europe: no more than four/five storeys, small alleys, people chatting, children playing. But there is no alignment of the buildings, no inner lanes and no perimeter walls. The city streets lead directly to buildings and to each dwelling. The situation is very different from the hierarchy of Chinese space.

Beside the space hierarchy, there is another clear and important difference between the two solutions. The direct relationship between the road and each apartment means that each one is "independent" of each other. The individual apartment buildings represent one living style solution. On the other hand, with the internal spaces — lanes, green areas, courtyards — each apartment joins the others in a community unit. The Shanghainese compound represents a different living style solution. The first comes from the Western tradition. The second comes from the Chinese tradition.

The Old Town and the Suzhou River areas are similar to the small town that I mentioned. Houses are not aligned, there is no perimeter wall, the public streets lead directly to each dwelling. These areas were not planned like the Longtang houses.

The Longtang house scheme came from the English terraced housing system. But — once more — the differences between the two demonstrates the differences between Western and Chinese living styles. The site plan for English terraced houses follows the site morphology and the urban layout. And furthermore each dwelling opens directly to the road. On the other hand, the Longtang houses are joined in a closed compound surrounded by a wall, and the positioning of each house is aligned only with the south.

Now I live in a modern compound in Hanghua Xincun, near the Hongqiao Airport. The layout and the living style are once again similar. Buildings are arranged in rows — one beside the other, one behind the other — all of them facing south. Even though each apartment is equipped with a heating system, the living room and the main room were planned on the south facade. The entrance is also on the south facade. A green area — where the children play and inhabitants chat — and the communal facilities (restaurant, gymnasium, swimming pool, children's playroom, etc.) are between the buildings. An iron fence surrounds the complex. The architecture is colorful and rich in detail (influenced by Western ideas). When the private shuttle-bus arrives from downtown, it stops in the center, in front of the communal building. People get off and others are waiting for them: it is similar to what happens in small towns in the countryside.

Alignment, south/north axis and style are very important symbols and architecture elements in Chinese tradition, not only in the past — for temples, Imperial Palaces and houses — but also in modern times for factories, houses, office buildings, hotels, etc. During these few years, I have noticed these Chinese concepts also in modern building design. When I designed a factory in Waigaoqiao Pudong, the Chinese owners and investors wanted the main entrance on the south side, even though the road on that side was a secondary one. The main road leading to the highway was on the north side, which in my opinion would have been more convenient for the movement of trucks.

In Shanghai, the most important factor is a choice of style for the new building and for the furniture inside. Every style is possible with no historical or taste limitation. It depends entirely on the owner or buyers' whim. Very often I have been asked to design a house in the European style. For me, this is nonsense. Maybe during Europe's Eclectic period, at the end of 19th century, the situation was similar: Gothic, Neo-classic, Renaissance, Vernacular, etc. People could choose what they wanted. Nowadays in

Shanghai thanks to its history, you can find — in existing buildings and in the choices for new ones — any style you want.

Recently I visited the work site of an old and important villa under restoration to be transformed into a guesthouse. The investors intend to furnish each room in different European traditional styles to give the "feel" of different environments, as in Las Vegas hotels.

But in recent times there are also new ideas. The new housing complex to be built along the Huangpu River will enjoy the riverfront. Designing a site plan nowadays, the main question concerns the main facade — and the best view: should it face south or the river? Follow the local tradition or follow imported international concepts?

Apart from these Chinese symbols, there are the international living style condominiums. Apartment buildings such as Taixing Apartments and Changde Apartments in the 1930s were, and Regent Tower, Chevalier Place and Gubei New Area in the 1990s are home mostly to foreigners and overseas. These structures are similar to what I was used to in Rome, built according to Western tradition. The buildings follow the street direction and do not strictly face south. The main entrance of the buildings is located on the road. There are no subsidiary passages between the public space (the road) and the private space (the apartment).

There is one more difference. A regular site plan brings peace to daily life thanks to its static urban composition. From each window, views are generally in the same direction: south. Everybody knows it. This comes from the Siheyuan house concept. The main hall faces south and the view of all the rooms is towards the central courtyard. There are no views of the city or of the outside. This means that nothing can be seen of the outside world from the house: only the sky (giving a timeless sensation). This was the situation in the Beijing hutongs and also in the Longtang houses in Shanghai. The modern Chinese compounds follow this tradition.

On the other hand, the irregular urban layout and different positioning of buildings generates an infinity of views. This is what happens in Western residential buildings. The "views" from the windows are infinite towards the environment, regardless of city or countryside. A multiplicity of unexpected views arising from a dynamic layout allows for a dynamic perception of the urban space. It recalls the Rotonda by Palladio: standing on the top of the hill it faces in four directions towards the countryside.

This is what I feel about living in Shanghai: two different housing solution concepts — and two different living styles — and ultimately two different means of construction. Regardless of the style of the building.

Bibliography Drawings and Old Photos

- Chen Congzhou, Tongji University,
  The History of Modern Architecture in Shanghai
  Shanghai Sanlian Press, 1988 (Chinese)
- *Controspazio n.3,* May/June 1992 monograph on Shanghai
  By Arch. Corrado Minervini, Turin and Prof. Zheng Shiling, Shanghai
  Gangemi Editore, Reggio Calabria 1992 (Italian)
- *Tour of Shanghai Historical Architecture*
  Henan Fine Arts Publishing House, 1994 (Chinese, English and Japanese)
- Luo Xiaowei, Tongji University, *A Guide to Shanghai Architecture*
  Shanghai People's Fine Arts Publishing House, 1996 (Chinese and English)
- Wu Jiang, *The History of Shanghai Architecture, 1840-1949*
  Tongji University Press, 1997 (Chinese)
- Luo Xiaowei, Wu Jiang, *Shanghai Longtang*
  Shanghai People's Fine Arts Publishing House, 1997 (Chinese and English)
- Zheng Shiling, Tongji University,
  The Evolution of Shanghai Architecture in Modern Times
  Shanghai Education Publishing House, 1999 (Chinese)
- Luigi Gazzola
  La casa della Fenice
  Diagonale, 1999 (Italian)
- Xue Shunsheng, Lou Chenghao
  Shanghai Ancient Buildings
  Tongji University Press, 2002 (Chinese)

Language Translation Notes

In this guide, Pinyin version is used for personal names and for the most used words. Pinyin is the transliteration from Chinese characters to Roman letters. The following are some examples of the translation from Pinyin to English:

Lu = Road   Bei = North
Nan = South   Zhong = Central
Dong = East   Xi = West
Longtang = a lane lined and terraced with residential houses
Shikumen = a style of houses having a wooden door with stone frames
Yi = One   Er = Two
Xizang = Tibet

PUTUO

CHANGNING

JING'AN

XUHUI

LUWAN

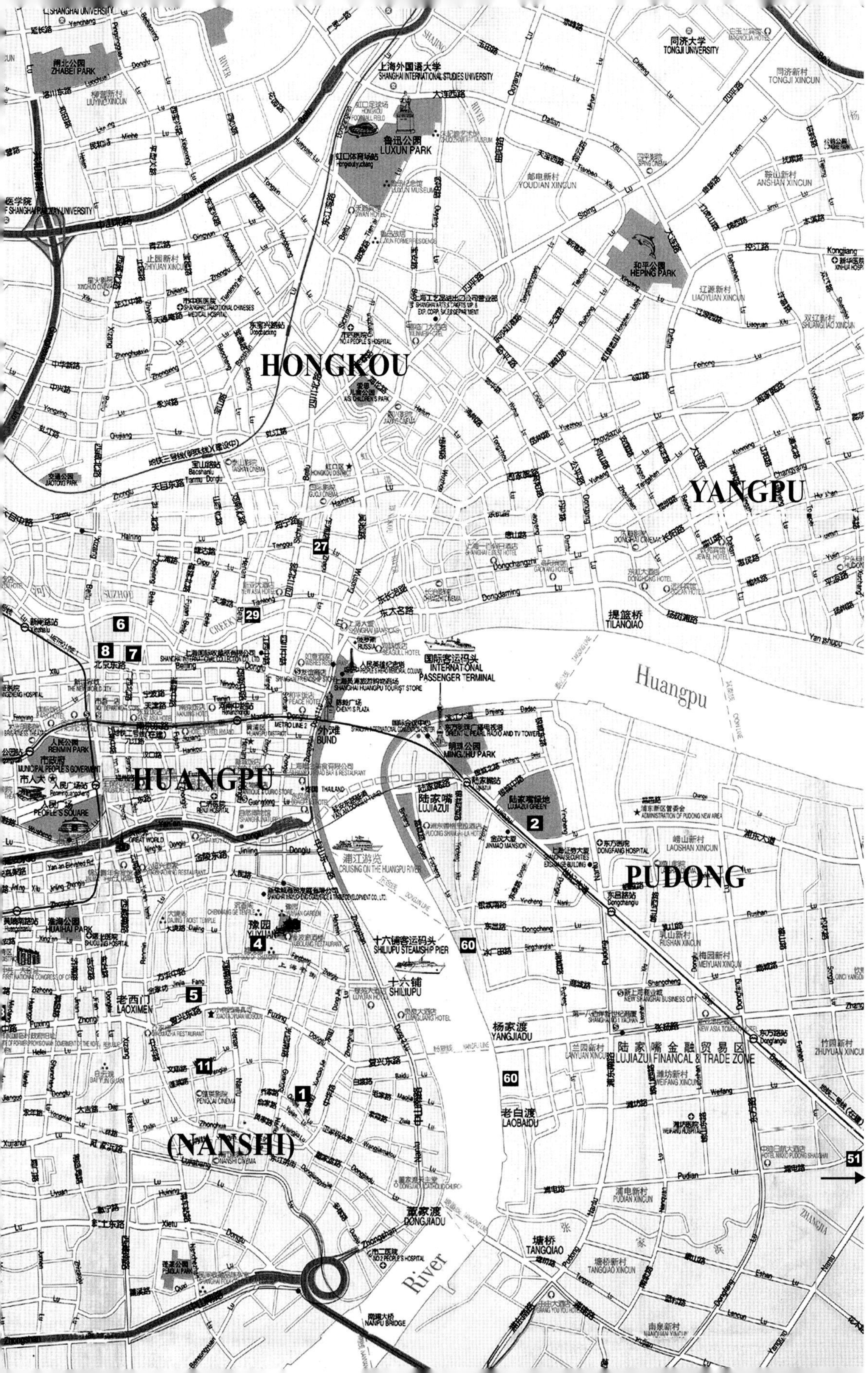
HONGKOU
YANGPU
HUANGPU
PUDONG
(NANSHI)
Huangpu
River
鲁迅公园
LUXUN PARK
和平公园
HEPING PARK
同济大学
TONGJI UNIVERSITY
上海外国语大学
SHANGHAI INTERNATIONAL STUDIES UNIVERSITY
闸北公园
ZHABEI PARK
国际客运码头
INTERNATIONAL PASSENGER TERMINAL
外滩
BUND
陆家嘴
LUJIAZUI
陆家嘴金融贸易区
LUJIAZUI FINANCIAL & TRADE ZONE
人民公园
RENMIN PARK
人民广场
PEOPLE'S SQUARE
豫园
YUYUAN
十六铺客运码头
SHILIUPU STEAMSHIP PIER
十六铺
SHILIUPU
浦江游览
CRUISING ON THE HUANGPU RIVER
杨家渡
YANGJIADU
老白渡
LAOBAIDU
董家渡
DONGJIADU
塘桥
TANGQIAO
南浦大桥
NANPU BRIDGE
提篮桥
TILANQIAO
老西门
LAOXIMEN
淮海公园
HUAIHAI PARK
1
2
4
5
6
7
8
11
27
29
51
60
60

Publisher: Zhang Ruizhi
Author: Luigi Novelli
Edition Editor: Lily Lijuan Zhou
Finalization: Eric Lock
Cover Design & Layout: Sinomedia

Shanghai Residential Buildings

Published by Haiwen Audio – Video Publishers
Printed by Shanghai Tenth Printing Co. Ltd.
Distributed by Shanghai Book Traders
390 Fuzhou Road, Shanghai 200001, China
First Edition: February, 2003
First Printing: February, 2003

Copyright © 2003 by Luigi Novelli and Shanghai Haiwen Audio-Video Publishers
All rights reserved. No part of this publication may be reproduced, stored in a retrieval system, or transmitted in any form or by any means, electronic, mechanical, photocopying, recording or otherwise, without the prior written permission of the Publisher.

Author's Notes:

Text and photos by the author. Totally 170 photos, 30 drawings for 60 buildings/complexes and 1 city map.

Except photos:
page 17 bottom — page 23 top and left — page 26 bottom and right — page 62 and 63 all — page 64 top — page 65 top — page 80 left — page 81 top right — page 82 — page 84 bottom